Mary Botham Howitt

Tales in Prose for Young People

Mary Botham Howitt

Tales in Prose for Young People

ISBN/EAN: 9783744686341

Printed in Europe, USA, Canada, Australia, Japan

Cover: Foto ©Thomas Meinert / pixelio.de

More available books at **www.hansebooks.com**

ABOUT A MAN AND A BEAR.—See Page 52.

TALES IN PROSE

FOR

YOUNG PEOPLE

BY

MARY HOWITT

New Edition

WILLIAM AND ROBERT CHAMBERS
LONDON AND EDINBURGH
1871

PREFACE

TO THE FIRST EDITION.

VERY little need be said by way of Preface to this volume of "Tales in Prose," except what is in grateful courtesy due to my friendly critics, who have so cordially and handsomely received its predecessor, "The Tales in Verse," and through whom it has at once obtained so extensive a circulation.

These very pleasing "Tales in Prose" having come into our possession, we have, so far as regards the appearance of the volume, endeavoured to do justice to the amiable and accomplished authoress.

W. AND R. CHAMBERS.

CONTENTS.

A NIGHT SCENE

IN A POOR MAN'S HOUSE.

A NIGHT SCENE

IN A

POOR MAN'S HOUSE.

It was the middle of winter, on the night of the twenty-third of January, when the weather was miserably cold; it neither decidedly froze, nor yet did it thaw; but between the two it was cold and damp, and penetrated to the very bone, even of those who sat in carpeted rooms before large fires, and were warmly clad. It was on this evening

that the seven little children of David
Baird, the weaver, stood huddled together in
their small room, beside a small fire, which was
burning comfortlessly. The baby lay in a
wooden cradle at one corner of the hearth.
The fire, to be sure, gave some warmth, because
it had boiled an iron pot full of potatoes, but it
gave very little cheeriness to the room. The
mother had portioned out the evening meal—
a few potatoes to each—and she now sat down
by the round table, lighted the farthing candle,
and was preparing to do some little piece of
housewifery.

"May I stir the fire?" asked David, the
eldest boy.

"No, no," replied the mother; "it burns
away too fast if it is stirred."

"I wish we had a good fire!" sighed Judith,
the second girl.

"Bless me!" said the mother, "it is a good
fire! Why, there's Dame Grundy and her
grandchild gone to bed because they have no
fire at all!"

"I should like some more salt to my potatoes," said little Bessy; "may I have some
more, mother?"

"There is none, child," she replied; "I put the last in the pot."

"O dear!" cried out little Joey, "my feet are so bad! They get no better, mother, though I did beat them with holly."

"Poor thing!" sighed the mother; "I wish you had better shoes."

"There's a pair," said Joey briskly, "at Timmy Nixon's, for fourteen-pence."

"Fourteen-pence!" repeated the mother; "it would take a long time to get fourteen-pence."

"Mat. Willis begged a pair of nice warm boots," replied Joey, experimentally.

"We will not beg," said the mother, "if we can help it—but let me see the shoes;" and Joey put up one of his miserably frost-bitten feet on his mother's knee. "Bless thee! my poor lad," said the mother, "thou shalt not go to work again till it is warmer."

"Mother," interrupted little Susan, "may I have some more?"

"There is no more," said she; "but I have a whole loaf yet."

"Oh dear, oh dear, how nice!" cried the children, clapping their hands; "and give Joey the bottom crust," said one, "because of his poor feet."

" And give me a big bit," cried Susan, holding out a fat little hand.

The mother divided the loaf—setting aside a piece for her husband—and presently the husband came.

" It rains, and is very cold," said he, shivering.

" Please God," rejoined the mother, " it will be warmer after the rain."

David Baird was a tall thin man, with an uneasy look—not that he had any fresh cause of uneasiness—his wages had not been lowered ; his hours of work had not been increased, nor had he quarrelled with his master ; but the life of a poor man is an uneasy life—a life of care, weariness, and never-ending anxieties. What wonder then, if his face have a joyless look ?

The children made room for their father by the fire ; Susan and Neddy placed themselves between his knees, and his wife handed him the portion of supper which had been set aside for him.

Mary, the eldest girl, was sitting on a box, feeding a squirrel with the bread which her mother had given her—she was very happy, and kissed the squirrel many times ; Judith was sitting beside her, and David held the cup out of which the squirrel drank.

"Nobody has inquired after that squirrel," said the father, looking at them.

"No," replied Mary, "and I hope nobody will."

"They will not now," said the younger David, "for it is three months since we found it."

"We might sell it for half-a-crown," said the father. Mary looked frightened, and held the squirrel to her bosom.

"Joey's feet are very bad," remarked the mother.

"And that doctor's bill has never been paid," said the father, "seventeen shillings and sixpence."

"'Tis more money than we get in a week," sighed the mother.

"I go round by the back-lane, to avoid passing the door," said the father, "and he has asked me for it three times."

"We will get it paid in the summer," rejoined the mother, hopefully; "but now coals are raised, and bread, they say, will rise before the week is out."

"Lord help us!" exclaimed the father.

"Mary, fetch the other candle," cried the mother, as the farthing candle burned low in the stick, and then went out.

"There is not one!" replied Mary; "we burned out the other last night."

"Have you a farthing, David?" asked the wife.

"Not one," replied he, rather hastily.

"Nor have we one in the house," said the wife; "I paid all we had for the bread."

"Stir up the fire then," said David.

"Nay," rejoined the wife, "coals are raised."

"Lord help us!" again sighed David, and two of the children began coughing. "Those children's coughs are no better!" remarked the father somewhat impatiently. And then the baby awoke, and so did Bessy, who had fallen asleep on the floor unobserved, crying: "I am so cold, mother; I am so cold!"

"Go to bed with her, Mary," said the mother, "for you were up betimes this morning, washing —put your clothes on the bed, and keep her warm."

Mary went into the little dark chamber to bed with her sister, and her mother tried to hush the crying infant.

David was distracted. He was cold, hungry, weary, and in gloom. Eight children whom he loved were about him, but he thought of them only as born to poverty, uneasiness, and care, like himself: he felt unhappy, and grew almost angry as the baby continued to cry.

Cheer up, David, honest man! there is that coming even now—coming within three streets' length of thee—which shall raise thee above want for ever! Cheer up! This is the last hour any of you shall want for fire—the last hour you shall want for candle-light. Thou shalt keep thy squirrel, Mary! Bessy, thou shalt have blankets to warm thee! The doctor's bill shall be paid—nor, David Baird, shalt thou ever again skulk by back ways to thy work to avoid an importunate creditor! Joey, thou shalt turn the wheel no longer—thy feet shall get well in woollen stockings, and warm shoes at five shillings a pair! You shall no more want salt to your potatoes, nor shall Susan again go short of her supper! But of all this, as yet, you know nothing, good people: and there you sit, hopeless and comfortless, and know nothing about the relief—and such splendid relief too—that even now is approaching your door. Wail,

little baby, an' thou wilt—nurse thy poor
tingling feet, Joey, by the fire; and muse in
sadness on thy poverty, David Baird, yet a few
moments longer; it can do you no harm, for the
good news is even now turning the corner of
your street.

Knock, knock, knock! David started from
his reverie.

"Some one is at the door," said the wife; and
up jumped little David. "If it is neighbour
Wood come to borrow some meal, you can get
her a cupful," added the mother, as the knock
was repeated more hastily.

Up rose David Baird, and, thinking of the
apothecary's bill, opened the door reluctantly.

"Are you David Baird?" asked the letter-
carrier, who had knocked.

"I am," said David.

"This, then, is for you; and there are twenty-
two pence to pay on it," said the man, holding
forth a large letter.

"Is it a summons?" cried the wife in dismay:
"for what is David Baird summoned?" and she
rushed to the door with the baby in her arms.

"It is no summons," replied the man, "but a
money-letter, I take it."

"It is not for me," said David, half glad to escape his liability to pay the two-and-twenty pence.

"But are you not David Baird the weaver?"

"I am," said David.

"Then," continued the letter-carrier, "pay me the twenty-two pence, and if it is not right they will return you the money at the post-office."

"Twenty-two pence!" repeated David, ashamed to confess his poverty.

"One shilling and tenpence," said the wife; "we have not so much money by us, good man."

"Light a candle," said the letter-carrier, bustling into the house, "and hunt up what you have."

David was pushed to an extremity. "We have none," said he; "we have not money to buy a candle!"

"Lord bless me!" said the letter-carrier, and he gave David the younger fourpence to fetch half a pound of candles. David and his wife knew not what to think; and the letter-man shook the wet from his hat. In a few moments the candles came, and the letter was put into David's hands.

"Open it, can't you?" said the letter-man.

"Is it for me?" inquired David again.

"It is," replied the other, impatiently—"what a fuss is here about opening a letter!"

"What is this?" exclaimed David, taking out a bill for one hundred pounds.

"Oh!" sighed the wife, "if, after all, it should not be for us! but read the letter, David!" and David read it.

"Sir—You, David Baird, weaver, of ——, and son of the late David Baird, of Marden-on-Wear, lineal descendant of Sir David Baird, of Monkshaughton Castle, county of York, and sole heir of Sir Peter Baird, of Monkshaughton aforesaid, lately deceased, are requested to meet Mr Dennis, solicitor, at York, as soon after the receipt of this as possible. It will be necessary for you to bring your family with you; and to cover travelling and other expenses, you will receive enclosed a bill for one hundred pounds, payable at sight.

"I have the honour to be,
"Sir,
"Your humble Servant,
"J. Smith, for Mr Dennis."

"Sure enough," said David, "David Baird, of Marden-on-Wear, was my father."

"Oh, oh, oh!" chuckled out little David, as he hopped about behind the group, "a hundred pounds and a castle!"

"Heaven be praised!" ejaculated the wife, while she hugged the baby in her arms.

"And," continued David, "the great Sir David Baird was our ancestor; but we never looked for anything from that quarter."

"Then the letter is for you?" asked the man.

"It is. Please Heaven to make us thankful for it," said David, seriously; "but," hesitated he, "you want the money?"

"No," said the letter-carrier, going out, "I'll call for that to-morrow."

"Bolt the door, wife," said David, as she shut the door after the man; "this money requires safe keeping."

"Mend the fire!" said the mother; and her son David put on a shovelful of coal, and raked out the ashes.

"Kiss me, my children!" exclaimed the father, with emotion; "kiss me, and bless God, for we shall never want bread again!"

"Is the house on fire?" screamed Mary, at the top of the stairs, "for there is such a blaze!"

"We are burning a mould candle," said Judith, "and have such a big fire!"

"Come here, Mary," said the father, and Mary slid down stairs, wrapped in an old cloak.

"Father's a rich man! we're all rich—and shall live in a grand castle!" laughed out young David.

"We shall have coats, and blankets, and stockings, and shoes!" cried Joey, all alert, yet still remembering his poor frost-bitten feet.

"We shall have roast-beef and plum-pudding!" said Susan.

"We shall have rice-pudding every day!" cried Neddy.

"And let me have a horse, father," said young David.

David Baird was again distracted; but how different were his feelings! He could have done a thousand extravagant things—he could have laughed, cried, sung, leaped about, nay, rolled on the floor for joy; but he did none of these —he sate calm, and looked almost grave. At length he said: "Wife, send the children to bed, and let us talk over this good-fortune together."

"You shall have all your Sunday clothes on to-morrow," said the happy mother, as she sent them up stairs. To bed they went, and after a while laughed and talked themselves to sleep. The father and mother smiled and wept by turns, but did not sleep that night.

Such sudden turns of fortune are not usual, and when they do occur, they are likely to do more harm than good. Let us hope that steady principle and a recollection of his poverty preserved David Baird from misusing the wealth he had so unexpectedly acquired.

A GIRL'S STORY.

A GIRL'S STORY.

My mother died when I was
young so as to have no recollection of her. My father was
captain of an Indiaman, and
was commonly out of England
for upwards of two years together. He was not

in the least wanting in affection towards me,
though he saw me so rarely, that I used to lose all
remembrance of his person in the intervals of
our meeting, and had, as it were, to commence
a new acquaintance with him every time he
returned, which was not a difficult thing to
do, for he was naturally fond of children, and
was fond of me to an extreme. As it happened
that there were no nearly-connected branches
of our family to whose care I could be intrusted,
my father placed me with an old woman who
had attended my mother most faithfully during
the long illness which ended in her death, and
to whose charge she had especially committed
me ; and, indeed, a kinder, better nurse never
lived than poor Mrs Bridget.

My father saw me gradually improving under
her care, from the little sickly baby my mother
left, to the strong, rosy child which he afterwards found me. As we lived in a secluded
village, remote from any considerable town,
but where my mother's property lay, I had not
the advantage of attending any good school.
Still, as the hamlet consisted of small farmers
and their labourers, I was looked upon as no
way inferior in learning or accomplishments to

any of them, though I was so utterly ignorant, that now I am frightened to think of it; for, of what was beyond the affairs and objects of our narrow, everyday life, I knew nothing— nay, even of these I knew, as it were, only the externals. I never reflected; I was only a mere animal, using its five senses, but no more; for of an intellectual or spiritual existence I knew as little as the fowls of the air. We were all as people having eyes, but seeing not; ears, but hearing not; and hearts, yet without compre- hension. I was, in most respects, like Peter Bell and the primrose, which

> A yellow primrose was to him,
> And it was nothing more.

To me, however, a flower had charms beyond the mere outside, and stirred sentiments within me which came and went, yet were not regarded. Generally speaking, all that surrounded me were but things with names. I learned their names, and then my knowledge ceased; but afterwards, when my mind was awakened, I was amazed at the ramifications, as it were, of know- ledge which spread from the commonest things that surrounded me; and then it was that I

found, to my infinite amazement, that glass, for
instance, was not the mere letters which spelled
the word *glass*, nor salt mere *salt*, but involved,
in a thousand ways, subjects of the most delightful interest. I was never tired of finding
knowledge in common things when I once knew
how. But how much more did all this apply
to my spiritual nature as connected with religious knowledge! I had been told that there
was a God—that I must repeat a form of words,
called prayers, morning and night, or that He
would be angry; that I must speak the truth,
or He would be angry also: in short, that I must
perform all my moral and religious duties to
avert His anger. I therefore had towards the
Divine Being no sentiment but that of undefined
fear. Here ended all my religious knowledge—
all was vague, dark, and unpleasing. Of love,
gratitude, and the filial reverence which the
human family owe to their heavenly Parent, I
knew nothing. This, my utter ignorance, my
father saw and deplored, nay, even tried to
remedy; but his visits were either too short, or
my nature too volatile, for any permanent
impression to be made by his instructions; and
spite of his earnest entreaties to Mrs Bridget,

that I might be properly taught in these matters, I made no progress whatever. And how, indeed, could I? for poor Mrs Bridget, with the best will in the world, was quite inadequate to the task. She was very ignorant, and, having weak sight, could scarcely spell out a chapter in the Bible—which, by some unaccountable chance, seemed always to open at a chapter of genealogy. Poor, dear soul! what sorrowful confusion she used to make when she tried to enlighten me in things she so dimly comprehended herself! Again, she was very rheumatic, and as the church had the reputation of being damp, and service was performed in it only every other Sunday, owing to the clergyman living at a distance, I had not the opportunity of attending divine worship, and thereby gaining some knowledge of holy things. Mrs Bridget, moreover, was a rigid churchwoman, and could not by any means have been prevailed upon to enter any of the dissenters' chapels; so that, from various causes, we seemed excluded from public worship altogether. She, however, kind soul! taught me all she knew, and that well. I could knit and sew, and was qualified in every respect for a notable housewife. I watched our

little meals cooking, when she was otherwise
occupied : I neatly mended my own clothes,
folded them up, and put them by with scrupu-
lous care. I even tried to wash, mounted in
my little pair of pattens to the wash-tub, and
was praised for my skill. I could iron without
either burning the clothes or my fingers ; and
was believed by my simple-minded guardian to
be as well-trained a little maiden as any in the
three next counties. ·

No child ever loved the .most tender mother
better than I. did my humble friend, and our
separation was a bitter pang, for I could not
foresee the happy consequences it would produce
to us both. But I am anticipating events.

At eight years old I was a tall, robust, ruddy
girl, with an immense quantity of curling chest-
nut hair dangling into my eyes and hanging
about my shoulders. I knew every field in the
parish, and every creature, tame and wild, that
might be found in them. In the summer I
went into the hay-fields to work or play, as I
liked best, and to ride in the empty wagons, or
tear my frock or my hands in gathering sprays
of wild roses, or long trailing stems of the
beautiful blue vetch. I was up with the earliest

dawn to pick mushrooms in the old pasture-fields; I went a-gleaning; I gathered black-berries, and spent whole days in picking bil-berries on a wide heath some miles off, with the poor children of the village, who gained their living at that season by doing so; and being instructed by Mrs Bridget to give my gatherings to my humble associates, I was, wherever I went, an honoured and welcome companion. There was not a man, woman, or child in the village that I did not familiarly know. Many a baby I had half nursed, and for many a little creature's untimely death I had sincerely mourned. These are small things to write about, and I tell them, not to make my young readers think too well of me, but as traits of my early character, training, and life; and if I add that I was generally beloved, let me not be thought vain, but do, my dear young readers, take into consideration, that among the poor people with whom I associated there was so much kindness, so much patient endurance of poverty and pain, and such unostentatious sym-pathising of poor neighbour with neighbour, that no one could have been, as I was, among them daily, nay, almost hourly, without having the heart improved, and the affections and charities of our nature called into activity, and thereby winning their confidence and love. Mrs Bridget was a most kindhearted, benevolent creature; and was enabled, by the allowance which was made for my maintenance, and our frugal way of living, to be a general benefactor. I was her almoner, and, through my intimate knowledge of every household, I became acquainted with all their wants and sorrows, which we had often the means, and always the will, to relieve. Oh! when I look back to those times, and see their happiness, their simplicity, and their humble usefulness, how do I mourn over the one fault which darkened it all—our ignorance of the true nature of spiritual things —even while our practice was, as to many outward matters, so truly Christian!

Although I was a considerable heiress in this country district, I knew little, and thought still less, about it. There was no parade about any thing. The honest farmer, who acted as my father's bailiff, quietly collected his yearly rents, transmitted them to his agent in town, paid our small, though amply-sufficient stipend, and there was an end of the matter. Our cottage stood on the farm of this good man. It was a sweet little spot, embosomed in trees, with a large garden, and a small orchard of old mossy trees, which, nevertheless, produced apples so red and so golden, that, in after-years, whenever I read of Hesperian apples, I saw, in fancy, those of our own orchard. Among the branches of the trees, and in their gnarled trunks, the robin, the chaffinch, the missel-thrush, the throstle, and the black-bird found warm and safe retreat; for in my predatory excursions I never harried the nest of any bird which, as it were, had put itself under our protection. At the bottom of the orchard ran a small winding brook, with broken banks, mossy and covered with every graceful and luxuriant plant that loves the water-side. The stream was shaded by alders, with here and there an immense half-decaying willow, which formed in itself a picturesque union of old age and vigorous youth. On the orchard slope grew snowdrops and wild daffodils, flowers which I can never see without the freshness and happiness of my early years returning with the memory of that green quiet orchard. Under the hedges, among the brown half-dissected leaves of the holly, sprung up the first violets of the year—violets, thickly set as the stars in the sky, white and blue, an almost inexhaustible succession, though my little basket was filled every morning.

Our garden was as old-fashioned as could well be conceived; we had no flowers but of the most primitive kind, but those in such luxuriant abundance as quite to make up for their inferior quality. Never did I see such clumps of crocuses as ours, nor such roots of polyanthuses; never such yellow and lilac primroses, nor elsewhere such roots of that old-fashioned oxslip, called by Mrs Bridget "dick-in-green-doublets." Poor Mrs Bridget loved her garden next to myself, and was very particular in the management of her auriculas, pinks, and carnations. Her horticulture was reckoned the finest in the country; and many an old neighbour came in on a Sunday evening, dressed in his best, to walk in our garden, and quietly compliment Mrs Bridget on the extraordinary excellence of her favourite flowers, or to beg a cutting or a root of one or the other, which the kind creature never refused.

It was a happy life I led. I had tame rabbits, pet robins, and a sparrow so remarkably tame as to sit perched on my finger, eat from my lip, come at my call, and nestle in my bosom to rest for hours together. I had a cat, and many families of kittens, and a terrier dog, called Badger, wonderfully ugly, as every body protested, but come, nevertheless, of so good a race, as to be in general request for every rat-catching and otter-hunting within many miles. I had strolled the country over in every direction, and was, in my vagrant and out-of-doors life, as bold and as independent, and as full of adventurous pleasure, as the most arrant gipsy that pitched her tent in our lanes. This life of freedom gave me the full use of all my limbs, and an energy and independence of character, which I found afterwards to be extremely useful, and which, in some degree, counterbalanced the defects of my early education.

Such was I, when my father announced his intention of visiting us, and for a longer period than usual. The tidings were those of great joy, for dear Mrs Bridget had always encouraged in my young heart the most ardent affection for my father; and, perfectly believing that she had entirely fulfilled her duty towards me, she anticipated his coming with impatience almost equal to my own. We talked of it morning, noon, and night; and such had always been the perfect integrity of her conduct, that now nothing was done differently in the prospect of my father's coming, nor was I instructed to do thus and thus, nor to say this or the other before him; for Mrs Bridget believed every thing had been done that he could desire, and exactly according to his wishes.

The first few days of my father's visit were days of unmingled pleasure : he found me grown beyond his hopes, and full of affection and buoyant spirits; and "all went merrily as a marriage bell" till Sunday, when, as there was that day no service at church, my father took me by the hand, and, seating me beside him on a little bench in the orchard, began to question me on religious subjects. He had been himself most religiously educated in his youth, and, I have heard it said, had performed family-worship for many years, with great solemnity and propriety, after his father's death, which occurred when he was but nine years old. He had always thought it of the highest importance that children should receive very early religious knowledge : it may therefore be imagined what

would be his horror to find me, though a
Christian's child, as ignorant as a little Pagan.
My answers to his questions, and my remarks,
were, I believe, painfully irrational or foolish ;
and I am ashamed to think how my ignorance,
which in the openness of my nature I fully
revealed, must have shocked and wounded his
deeply religious mind.   Never shall I forget
the agony of my spirit, when I saw him burst
into tears, and bewail over me as a lost,
neglected creature.   The sudden sense of a
great calamity fell upon me, and I felt as if
I had in some way betrayed a fatal secret,
which would bring misery on dear Mrs Bridget,
for I heard my father couple her name with
epithets which, though I could not fully understand them, I knew to be terms of reproach and
displeasure.   After some time, he took me again
by the hand, and returned with me to the
house, where he poured out his great anger
against the amazed Mrs Bridget.   She had
warm feelings, loved me better than her life,
and, believing me a faultless creature, was no
less hurt than angry at my father's reproaches.
The end of this strange and distressing scene
was my father's determination to remove me

from her guardianship ; and, spite of my prayers
to remain, and Mrs Bridget's tears, expostula-
tions, and upbraidings, she was ordered to pack
up my little wardrobe and prepare me for a
journey on the morrow.   What an unhappy
evening that was !   I sat like one stupified
with some strange sorrow, and many, many
times half believed it a painful dream, from
which I tried in vain to wake.   Nothing in the
world, I am sure, could have prevailed on poor
Mrs Bridget to make the needful preparations,
but the knowledge that I must be the sufferer
if she neglected to provide comfortably for the
journey, which, she was told, would be a long
one.

I will not attempt to tell my young readers
what a melancholy going-to-bed mine was that
night—how the dear, kind creature wept over
me, and kissed me, and folded me in her arms—
looking in my face with the most passionate
love, and then hiding hers in her apron to con-
ceal her grief.   I laid myself down upon the
bed where we had so often slept together, and
burying my face in the pillow, cried myself into
an uneasy slumber.   In the very early morning
I awoke.   All was still in the house, except the

crickets, which I heard chirping on the kitchen hearth—but no Mrs Bridget was in bed! I started up half terrified, and drawing the curtain aside, saw, by the light of the moon, the kind creature sitting in the room, her face covered with both her hands, and presently after heard the sobs which she could no longer restrain. She had been busy all the night making preparation for my journey; and now, while some little confectionery was baking in the oven, she had stolen up to be near me while I was yet under the same roof.

The remainder of the night I did not sleep, but at my earnest request, I was carried down to the warm kitchen hearth, where, after being dressed with the most solemn care, and wrapped in her best scarlet cloak, we sat down to pass the time together, with protestations of affection, and with many tears, till the early hour which was fixed for my departure.

In the morning my father seemed softened towards my poor friend. He permitted our tediously-long parting without impatience, and even wept himself, to witness the vehement sorrow of the poor old woman, to whom, in truth, both he and I owed so much.

c

Our journey was a very long one; and, finally, I was placed under the care of a widow lady of the name of Herman, an early friend of my father, and who, having lost several young children of her own, was willing to receive me in the place of a little daughter. I am ashamed to confess that I was so wretched at parting from dear Mrs Bridget, that I closed my heart against any one who might be chosen to supply her place, and wickedly determined not to love her, nor even to make myself amiable to her. But the soul of a child so used to affection as I had been could not long remain insensible to daily and hourly kindness; I felt it instinctively in the tone of Mrs Herman's voice, in the expression of her countenance, and could as little resist its influence as the opening of the flowers could resist the sunshine. In a few days, therefore, we were better friends than it had been my intention that we ever should become. She knew all the peculiar circumstances of my young life from my father, and having won my confidence, soon penetrated my heart also, and in so doing, learned much that made her admire my poor, humble friend. She encouraged me to talk about her, and on this subject I never was weary. What was my surprise, when one day, after such a conversation, she remarked to my father, on his entering the room, that she hoped he would allow Mrs Bridget to take up her residence with us, and still be my attendant, though under her own inspection. My father seemed amazed, and even for a moment objected; but she pleaded so kindly for the poor old woman, urging our many obligations to her, and hoping that we might be the means of instructing her on subjects of which she seemed so ignorant, that in the end my father consented. I was overpowered by this goodness, and clasping my arms round Mrs Herman's neck, shed tears of joy and gratitude. The next day my father again set off to our village to bring back with him my kind and early friend.

Mrs Bridget was still more endeared to me by this short separation, and never was child so happy in the prospect of any pleasure as I was in this reunion. I fancied to myself how she would look, and what would be the dress in which she would arrive—the handsome chintz gown and fine linen apron, the scarlet cloak, and the black mode bonnet, trimmed with old-fashioned black lace. I described her over and

over again to my new friend, and even told
what she would assuredly say at our first meeting. But I was wrong. My father found her
ill in bed—ill, as the doctor averred, from
excessive grief; and although she rose up, as
soon as she heard the glad tidings, declaring
that she was able to undertake the journey that
very day, it was too much for her, and I had to
receive her a feeble invalid.

All the household was affected by her arrival,
and the most unwearied kindness and attention
were bestowed upon her. These things all
touched the good heart of Mrs Bridget ; and she
who, like me, had entered the house with preju-
dice against its inmates, could not· be proof
against their kindness.

My father did not remain with us long enough
to witness her recovery and establishment in
the family. To her was intrusted the care of
my person and clothes, to which she had so
long zealously attended. She had a little room
of her own, and the allowance which was made
to her formerly being still continued, made her
a rich woman.

Now began, indeed, the golden days of my
life. The Bible which had been hitherto a

sealed book to us both, lay open before us, and
the joy of my life was to sit at dear Mrs Bridget's
knee, and read to her the simple, beautiful, and
affecting narratives it contains. In her mind
there was nothing to counteract the influence
of good; she received it with the sincerity and
simplicity of a little child, and with the knowledge she thus gained, sentiments awoke in her
soul of which she had but little idea before. Poor,
dear Mrs Bridget, what an insatiable delight
had she in those pleasant ancient stories—nor
was the pleasure I took in them less than hers!
With what amazement and love did we read the
history of Joseph—his being torn from his
doting father came home to her heart! The
exploits of David—the lives and deeds of Elisha
and Elijah—the true-heartedness and affection
of Ruth—the integrity and wonderful deliver-
ance of the three faithful children from the
burning fiery furnace, and of Daniel from the
lions' den; but, above all, the history of the
Shunamite woman and her little son—and of
David and the lost child of his affections, were
full of the most engrossing interest to her; and
in all she found something to which her own
heart and its experience responded. But if I

first pointed out these extraordinarily interesting histories to the dear old creature, it was she who first awoke my mind to the beauty, the purity, the benevolence, and the heroism of the character of our Saviour.

It was a pleasant life that we now led! Mrs Herman always encouraged me to converse on these subjects, and to me they were the most delightful and the most interesting that we ever spoke upon ; for she made religion so lovely, by the cheerfulness of her conversation, that I could not believe any one could ever shrink from it as a gloomy subject.

Thus passed over several years. In the meantime I was learning a variety of things which it was necessary for me to know—geography, and the natural history and manners of the inhabitants of the eastern countries, among the rest. These I found wonderfully to elucidate my knowledge of the Scripture histories, and I aspired to teach Mrs Bridget the same ; but here, poor dear soul, she was as dull as a block, and seemed to comprehend nothing about them. Her heart was not interested by them, and all Mrs Bridget's knowledge must pass through her affections. I therefore left her to the Bible alone, while I read and studied various other books and histories, and gained as much information as satisfied my friends, if not myself.

I need not pursue the subject further. My kind young readers, who have gone thus far with me, will be sure that the latter days of poor Mrs Bridget were made as happy as possible—they were so indeed! She lived to a good old age, and then, full of love and peace, passed to that brighter world for which the knowledge of her latter years had so worthily prepared her.

ANECDOTES.

HOW A MAN COULD CATCH "WILL-O'-THE-WISP."

THERE was a man, once upon a time, and within the memory of several old people now living, who was bent upon catching Will-o'-the-Wisp, or, as it is sometimes called, Peg-with-her-lantern. Nobody but himself believed he could do this; but he was himself quite sure he could accomplish it, and whenever he had an extra glass of ale, he was always ready to set out on the expedition. It happened therefore, one night, as he came from Denby, a village in Derbyshire (the village where Flamstead, the astronomer, was born), not remarkably sober, and yet steady enough to keep his ground, he resolved to make the attempt. What he meant to do with Peg when he caught her I do not know; perhaps he did not exactly know himself; nor am I sure that he had any idea what sort of a thing she would prove; but mystery, some people think, makes things more interesting, and so, I suppose, it was in his case. On he went, therefore, towards some old fishponds, where there was a long and wide morass; and immediately, as if fortune would favour him, he descried the object of his desire, glimmering out before him. Off he went, floundering and plunging like a wild horse, through bog and over bush; but, when he had reached the spot, she had vanished, and again gleamed out before him like a little spark, at the distance of a hundred yards. But, as he expected to have some trouble in taking her, he was not to be easily daunted, and vowing to make sure of her at last, off he went again. Peg, however, as wild and nimble as her brother Jack-o'-lantern, had set off again as far away to the right hand. To the right, therefore, he went; but when he got there, through bush, through brake, off she had skipped away to the left, and he, nothing dismayed, went off, like a bold hunter, in that direction. Peg now seemed in a much quieter

and steadier humour, and the nearer he came
the brighter she gleamed and glimmered—now,
for a moment, dimming herself, then again
shining out clearer than ever. Our pursuer,
certain of the prize, threw off his coat, which
had somewhat impeded his motions, and chuckling to himself over the prize he was about to
win, sprang forward with outstretched arms to
seize her, uttering an exultant shout of " Now I
have you !" and plunged his arms up to his
shoulders in a peat-fire !

OF A RAVEN THAT WENT
TO A FAIR.

THERE was, some fifty years ago, a cunning and
mischievous raven, named Ralph, kept at a
lonesome farmhouse in Derbyshire. He was a
great favourite with all the family, though he
often created much annoyance and trouble by
his thievish tricks. Whatever came in his way,
which was not too heavy for him to lift, he
carried off; yet, though every one knew who
was the thief, he seldom came in for punishment, the servants and different members of the
family being blamed instead, for leaving things
in his way. Notwithstanding the care, however,
which everybody took to put things in their
places, Ralph found many a little article of

which he made prize, and many a one which
was never missed at the time.

After Ralph had practised his thievery, and
indulged his habit of secretiveness for some
years, all his hoard came one day suddenly to
light. He had buried it in, as he had thought,
a cunning hole that he had made in the thatched
roof of a barn. His treasures grew and grew,
and the hole had been deepened and deepened,
till it was as deep as the thatch itself, and then
all his accumulation fell through upon the barn
floor. And what a wonderful accumulation
there was!—thimbles, small pieces of money,
balls of cotton, knitting-needles, curtain-rings,
one or two gold rings, a brooch, sleeve-buttons,
two salt-spoons, a mustard-pot lid, a seal and
the gold-setting of a seal, combs, little old
housewives, pincushions, buckles, hair-pins, and
all the multitude of small things that abound
in the houses of tolerably well-conditioned
people. There was a world of amusement in
the owning of Ralph's treasury, and many an
old-forgotten thing was brought to light, and
many another was found of which nobody could
give any account.

The winter after this event, poor Ralph came

to an untimely end. The travelling tailor who used to come now and then to the house, to make and mend the clothes of the family, had made him, of scarlet cloth, a comb and wattles, like those of a chanticleer, which he allowed to be put on, and seemed to wear with as much pride as a young soldier wears his new uniform. Not long after being thus accoutred, there chanced to be a fair in the neighbourhood, and, as several members of the family went to it, Ralph saw no reason why he might not go also. Off, therefore, he flew after them, and arriving in the height of the fair, perched upon the roof of a house which stood in the centre of the bustle. The poor fellow had all his bravery on, and was immediately descried, everybody taking him for some wonderful bird, and everybody being desirous of securing him.

Unfortunately, a man with a gun was at hand, and, to make sure of so strange a creature while he was within reach, fired at him, and poor Ralph and his bravery fell together. Hardly had he reached the ground, when his old friends of the farm came up with a crowd that had been drawn to the spot by the firing of the gun, and in the strange nondescript creature they instantly recognised their old favourite. Great was the lamentation that was made over him, and loud and vehement their indignation at the impatient rabble who had so summarily ended his days. His sagacity was an endless theme of discourse; story after story was told of him, and so great was the sympathy of all the fair-going people, that for some time they forgot the amusements that surrounded them, to condole over the unfortunate raven that came to the fair in all his finery to meet so tragic an end.

HOW A BULLFINCH DIED OF JOY.

THERE was once a bullfinch kept by a lady, which was so extremely fond of her as to exceed any instance of attachment I ever heard of before. Her presence created a sort of sunshine to him, and he sang and rejoiced with his whole heart when she was by ; while he drooped in her absence, and would sit silent in his cage for whole days together.

The lady fell sick, and was confined to her bed for a week with so severe an illness, as to be entirely disabled from thinking of the bird. At length, when she was sufficiently recovered to see him, she ordered his cage to be brought and set upon the bed beside her. The poor bird knew her voice in an instant, though it was weak and low from her extreme fever.

The cage-door was opened ; he uttered a shrill cry between a song and a scream—fluttered from her hand to her cheek, and then fell down, dead !

ABOUT A MAN AND A BEAR.

WHEN I was wandering in the backwoods of
North America (said a traveller), I came one
day upon an old man, the most picturesque
object I ever saw; his dress was of coarse home
manufacture, and was rudely shaped to his
large-boned person, probably by the hand of
some female tailor. His clothes were torn by
wandering among forests, and literally hung
about him in shreds and tatters; and, amid
the various parts of his wearing-apparel, several
little articles of Indian manufacture were to be
seen. Over his deer-skin leggings he wore the
curiously-wrought moccasins, or Indian shoes:
in the place of a hat, he had a scarlet wampum-
belt bound round his head, and he smoked from
an Indian pipe. Notwithstanding this curious

costume, his countenance shewed at a glance
that he belonged to civilised society; and his
friendly salutation, spoken in good English,
sounded delightful to me, after having ceased
to hear my native tongue for many weeks.

The old man sat upon a fallen tree, and
seemed to have just taken his repast; for his
dried venison and Indian bread, and yet open
wallet, lay before him. I needed no second
invitation to partake his seat; and drawing
forth my own store of provision, followed his
example.

My old man of the woods was a surveyor,
employed by the American government to
measure and set out tracts of land in the back-
settlements. It was a wild and lonely life that
he led, and one which afforded him continual
opportunity of gaining knowledge of Indian
life and character, and of observing the habits
of the beasts and birds of the wilderness.

The bears, he told me, were the most trouble-
some neighbours he had in his out-of-doors life;
and he said that he was obliged to hang the
wallet containing his provisions in a tree while
he slept, otherwise these audacious creatures
would steal it, even from under his head. He

was sleeping, he said, one night, with his wallet
for his pillow, when he was awoke by something
violently tugging at it. He started up, and
saw in the early dawn a shaggy black bear:
he rose, and opening his bag, threw him a large
piece of his dried venison, saying : " There,
take that, and welcome ! " The bear snapped
it up, and then stood waiting for more : he
threw him another piece, saying : " Take that,
then, and prithee, begone ! " Again the bear
stood in expectation. A third time he threw
him a slice, exclaiming : " Why, thou 'st no
conscience ; take that, and be satisfied ! " But
the bear, still insatiable, gulped down the third
piece with a great swallow, and again stood
waiting for more. At this the man's patience
came to an end, and heaving up his great staff,
he gave him a lusty blow on his head, bellowing
at the highest pitch of his voice : " Take *that*,
then, and be off with thee ! " Upon this the
bear, uttering a loud cry, trotted away into the
woods, and the old man saw no more of him ;
but, after this adventure, he took care to hang
his provisions far enough out of the reach of
the bears.

OF A DOG THAT COULD AND COULD NOT RECKON TIME.

MANY persons think that dogs, however sagacious, have no notion of the recurrence of
periods of time, unless they are guided by
external signs; as, for instance, the return of
the Sunday by the cessation of the week's
labour. But there was a dog which was guided
by something beyond this in his calculation of
times, and of him I am about to give an anec-
dote. He was a white terrier of a good race,
and his name was Pry, and, though active and
clever in the pursuit of vermin, not remarkably
gifted with any great intellectual powers. He
belonged to a family of the Society of Friends,
who lived in a country place, and who were in

the habit of attending their meeting—their
week-day meeting, as they called it—on the
Thursday, some two miles off, in a lonely and
rather wild place. Pry took it into his head
that he, too, would attend the meeting: it was
famous sport for him to run up and about
the wild hollows and deep lanes and water-
courses that lay between his home and the
meeting-house; and such an amusement, once
a week, would not have been denied to him, had
he been contented to stay quietly in the stable
with the horses, or lie outside the door till his
master was ready to return home. But Pry
had a will of his own, and he chose to lie at
his master's feet in summer, and before the
warm stove in winter, while the Friends continued their sitting together; and though it
must be acknowledged that his behaviour was
unexceptionable, still it was looked upon as
somewhat indecorous to introduce a dog into
so grave a company. The family, therefore,
well knowing the pertinacity of Pry's temper,
gave orders that he should be tied up on
meeting mornings, and. thus kept at home
perforce. For a week or two this was done,
to poor Pry's great discomfort; but at length

he outwitted them. On these mornings he was
never to be found, so that he secured his own
liberty, and then joined his master about half-
way on the road, or rather kept him in view,
and demurely followed him to the place of
worship. After a little time longer, when he
supposed the discipline to have somewhat
relaxed—though he would never venture his
liberty within the house on these especial
mornings, not even to come for his breakfast—
he took his station at the top of the village
street, within sight of the door and windows
of his master's house, and there patiently waited
till he saw signs of setting out, and then trotted
on in great security and good-humour. When
Pry's master saw, by all these stratagems, and
all this doggish wisdom, that he was bent upon
his purpose, he made no further opposition, and
Pry became a regular and authorised attender
of Friends' meetings. But now comes the sin-
gularity of the story. About once in every two
months the meeting was held at a distant place,
which the family but rarely attended. The dog
knew when the regular day of the week recurred,
and invariably set out, trotting by himself to
the very meeting-house door, which, when he

found shut, he examined with a curious kind of canine wonderment ; and then, after having walked over the grave-yard, and round and into the stable, without finding any token of arrival, sedately turned back again, and though apparently perplexed and disappointed, soon set his nose to the ground, and traced out all the wonders of the homeward way.

Now, that a dog should know when it was the meeting-day by some external signs, as the bringing up of a horse, the putting on of his master's gaiters, or perhaps by the conversation of the family, does not seem so extraordinary, considering the wonderful instances of canine acuteness which we have on record; but that he should actually know, without ever mistaking it, when the day came—though there was no outward sign of preparation—nor even conversation about it—certainly was singular. The dog, though he had intellect enough to know the recurring day in seven, had yet not sufficient intellect to discover the regular exception, which happened about every eighth week.

OF A RAVEN THAT HAD A DINNER-PARTY.

THERE was a raven kept, a few years ago, at Newhaven, at an inn on the road between Buxton and Ashbourn. This bird had been taught to call the poultry, and, like the parrot of Paraguay, could do it very well too. One day—the table being set out for the coach-passengers' dinner—the cloth was laid, with the knives and forks, spoons, mats, and bread, and in that state it was left for some time, the room-door being shut, though the window was open. The raven had watched the operation very quietly, and, as we may suppose, felt a strong ambition to do the like.

When the coach was just arriving, the dinner

was carried in; but, behold! the whole para-
phernalia of the dinner-table had vanished—
silver spoons, knives, forks—all gone! But
what was the surprise and amusement to see,
through the open window, upon a heap of rub-
bish in the yard, the whole array very carefully
set out, and the raven performing the honours
of the table to a numerous company of poultry
which he had summoned about him, and was
very consequentially regaling with bread!

HOW A BOY TOOK A FLIGHT.

THERE is a story, and which I believe is a fact, of two boys going to take a jackdaw's nest from a hole under the belfry-window in the tower of All-Saints' Church, Derby. As it was impossible to reach the nest while standing within the building, and equally impossible to ascend to that height from without, they determined to put a plank through the window, and, while the heavier boy secured its balance by sitting on the end within, the lighter boy was to fix himself on the opposite end, and from that perilous situation to reach the object of their desire. So far the scheme answered according to their wishes. The little fellow took the nest, and finding in it five fledged young birds, announced the news to his companion.

"Five, are there?" replied he; "then I'll have three!"

"Three!" exclaimed the other indignantly. "No; I ran all the danger, and I will have the three."

"You shall not," still maintained the boy in the inside—"you shall not. Promise me three, or I'll drop you!"

"Drop me, and welcome," replied our little hero; "but I will promise you no more than two."

The boy inside slipped off the plank, the end tilted up, and down went the lesser boy upwards of a hundred feet to the ground. At the moment of his fall he was holding his prize by the legs, two in one hand and three in the other, and the birds finding themselves descending, instinctively fluttered out their pinions. But it was not these alone which saved the boy. He had on a stout new carter's frock, secured round the neck, and this, filling with air from beneath, buoyed him up like a balloon, and he descended smoothly to the ground, alighting, like a cat, on his legs; and then, looking up, he exclaimed

to his companion : " Now, you shall have none ! "
and. ran. away, sound in limb, to the astonishment of the inhabitants, who, with inconceivable
horror, had witnessed his descent.

HOW A JEST WAS NO JOKE.

WHEN I was a little child of five or six years old, I and my sister, rather older than myself, were taken by our father to spend a summer's day in Needwood Forest. We were little wild things, as brown and as hardy as gipsies, and many a long happy day we had spent under the forest trees, dining in woodmen's cottages, or, if none were at hand, by the side of a little running stream in some old woodland hollow.

Towards noon, on one of these happy days, as we were wearied with a long morning's ramble, we were left to recover from our fatigue under the spreading shade of an immense tree, like fairies in a fairy tale ; looking as diminutive as they in proportion to this giant of the forest, and being almost lost among its curled

and twisted roots, which were heaved up, old
and mossed and rugged, and wreathed together
like a nest of angry snakes, which had been
turned to stone ages and ages before. Around
us lay a small opening of forest glade, covered
with short green grass, upon which the sunshine
fell with such soft light, as to give it the colour
of clear emerald; this was enclosed by thickets
of black holly, which, in contrast with the light
foreground, looked still more intensely dark;
under and among these grew the greenwood-
laurel with its clusters of poisonous-looking
berries, and whole beds of the fair, white stel-
laria, shining like stars (whence its name)
among its grass-like leaves of tender green.
In other spots grew clusters of the dark, mys-
terious-looking enchanter's nightshade, and the
singular and rare four-leaved Herb-Paris, or
True-love, bearing its berry-like flower at the
central angles of its four leaves.

There was an undefined feeling, half of pleasure and half of pain, in being left alone in so
wild a spot. We heard the crow of the distant
pheasant, the coo-coo of the wood-pigeon, and
the laugh-like cry of the woodpecker; and
these, though familiar to us, seemed strangely

E

to add to the solitariness of the scene. And
yet it was very delightful. We talked cheerfully of everything around us; watched the

hare run past, or from thicket to thicket; and
the starling creep up the old trees, and the little

birds fly in and out from their woody screens with more than common interest. But at length, after long watching and long observation, we remarked to each other a strange, unceasing, low sound, which we could not comprehend; it seemed to keep up a perpetual chirr-chirr-r-r-ing somewhere near us, but exactly where we could not tell. At times it appeared just beside us, and then half the glade's distance off; now it was high, now low, now on this side, now on that—the strangest, most perplexing, and incomprehensible sound we had ever heard.

In the midst of our wonderment and lack of counsel, up came a stout forest-boy, of twelve years or thereabouts. He was a brown and wild-looking creature, like a very satyr of the woods; he was dressed in a suit of leather, had a belt round his waist, in which he carried his wood-knife, and on his back was a bundle of fagots. As he came up, he seemed amazed to find two children, like the Babes in the Wood, seated hand in hand at the foot of an old tree, and made a pause to look at us. We were not alarmed at his strange appearance, for such figures, in such grotesque garbs, were familiar to us in our forest wanderings; so, hailing him as a friend and counsellor, we demanded what was that strange, low voice which we heard somewhere thereabout.

The boy looked at us for half a moment with a sort of grin, and then, with a sudden look of fear, half bending his body, and speaking in a low but distinctly-articulated whisper: "It's my Lord Vernon's blood-hounds," said he ; "they are out hunting, and yon sounds are the chains which they drag after them !" and so saying, he dashed off like a wild stag.

What a horror now fell upon us! The glade was like an enchanted forest: all at once the trees seemed to swell out to the most gigantic and appalling size ; every twisted root seemed a writhing snake, and every old wreathed branch a down-bending adder ready to devour us. The holly thickets seemed full of an increasing blackness, which, like a dreadful dream, appeared growing upon our imagination till it was too horrible to be borne. We felt as if hemmed in by a mighty wilderness of gloom that cut us off from our kindred; and still the chirr-r-chirr-r of the terrible hounds, and their draggling chains, sounded through the dreadful silence, and seeming to our affrighted senses to come nearer and nearer, well-nigh drove us distracted. What, indeed, would have become of us, I know not, had we been left to ourselves and our terrors; but our cry of "Father! father!" speedily brought him to us, and the enchantment fled with his presence. The laugh with which he heard our story dispelled the whole terror of it. "It is the grasshopper and nothing more," said he, "which has caused all this foolish alarm;" and then, listening for a moment, he traced it by its sound among the short, dry sunny grass, and then held it in his hand before us. "And yet he was a wicked boy," continued our father, "who told a falsehood to frighten you thus. But come, now you shall go to your dinner;" and so saying, and taking one by each hand, he led us from the enchanted glade to a woodman's cottage in the next dell.

MATTHEW NOGGINS'
LETTER TO HIS COUSIN.

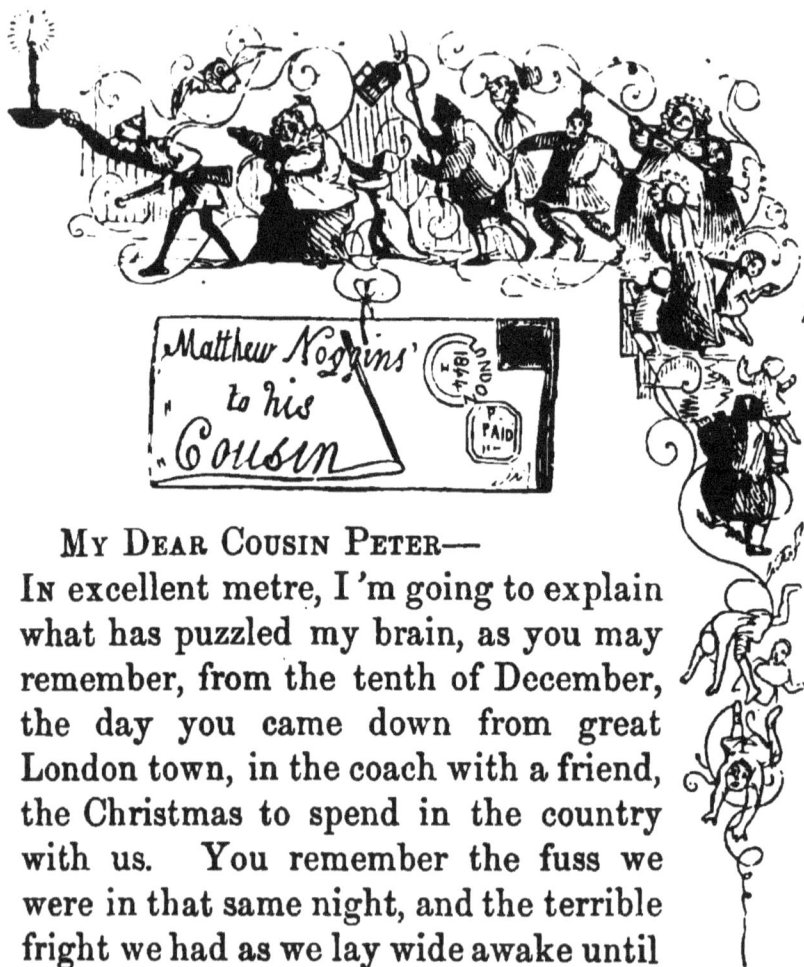

My Dear Cousin Peter—
In excellent metre, I'm going to explain
what has puzzled my brain, as you may
remember, from the tenth of December,
the day you came down from great
London town, in the coach with a friend,
the Christmas to spend in the country
with us. You remember the fuss we
were in that same night, and the terrible
fright we had as we lay wide awake until
day, wond'ring what was the matter, because of
the clatter there was in the house; neither cat.

rat, nor mouse, nor dozens of any, nor ever so many, we were sure could have made that wild cannonade.

And you haven't forgot, I'm sure you have not—how Sam, like a ghost, stood at the bed-post, as white as a sheet, trembling down to his feet, and praying that we would go with him, and see what that terrible rout could be all about. Then you know how we went, with courageous intent, all three on tip-toe, above and below; how we peeped into presses and tumbled o'er dresses—how we looked under beds and poked in our heads, to many a room full of silence and gloom; how we stole to the kitchen to see if the witch in a kettle or pan had cunningly ran. Then you know how my mother cried out: "What a pother is this that you make! One would think an earthquake shook the house o'er our heads; go all to your beds! 'Tis nothing at all but the wind in the wall, or a strange cat got in that has made such a din!"

Then to bed we did creep, but it was not to sleep, for I certainly think that not one got a wink; but asleep or awake, we were all in a quake, and rejoiced when the day sent the darkness away. And at breakfast you know,

how old Mrs Snow and Mrs Germain told the
tale of Cock-lane, and many another such tale
to my mother, and all looked so queer, betwixt
wonder and fear, that we very well knew that
all of them too had had a good fright, upon the
last night, as well as ourselves, whom they
called " silly elves." But you know, after this,
there was nothing amiss, and the nights were as
still as the top of a hill, where there cannot be
heard e'en the chirp of a bird : and so ever
after 'twas subject of laughter.

But Peter, my friend, just read to the end,
and then you shall know what chanced two
nights ago.

When all were asleep, just as day 'gan to
peep, about three of the clock, ere the crow of
the cock, we were waked, one and all, by a
rattle and squall, and a rumbling and jumbling,
as if things were tumbling right over our heads;
or as if on the leads loads of stones had been
hurled ; or the end of the world was certainly
coming, with thumping and drumming, and
running about, the most horrible rout—with
the squall of a cat and the cry of a bird, such a
racket as ne'er out of Bedlam was heard !

Well, you may be sure, this could not endure

without in a flurry and very great hurry all
running to see what the matter could be. And
Martha and Jane, and stout Adam Blanc, and
old Thomas and I, we determined to try if we
could not find out what the noise was about ; so
up stairs and down we went over the house, and
left not a corner to harbour a mouse. The old
clock was ticking, the crickets were clicking ;
the little canary hung up in the dairy, and the
guinea-pig lay fast asleep in the hay, and there
was not a trace of a thing out of place. But
just at the moment, when we had got no scent,
again it was heard, so loud, on my word, that
we started each man, and the women looked
wan, with a terrified stare, as they whispered
" 'Tis there !" Then old Thomas Baffin did
straight fall a-laughing, and bade us all follow ;
and off with a " Hollo ! " ran up the back stairs,
shouting : " I 'll give you bones to rattle like
stones ! You dog and you cat, what would you
be at !" Says Martha to Jane : "Why, he 's
mad, and that 's plain ! let 's go up to Missis,
and say how strange this is !" But I answered:
" Oh no, you shall not do so, you would frighten
my poor mother out of her wits ; why, you look
as if both were just falling in fits—what a couple

of cowards you are to be sure! Nay, stay by
the fire if you dare go no higher, and Adam and
I will go up and spy what this horrible riot and
racket can be."

Now mark, you are told that I looked very
bold; but Peter, my dear, let me say in your
ear that I certainly felt as if going to melt; for
I heard such a battering, such thundering and
clattering, and Thomas a-calling, as if for help
bawling, that I felt half inclined to alter my
mind, and not back the fellow, howe'er he might
bellow.

But on with my letter—my pride got the
better—so bidding my cowardice go to the wall,
I up stairs ascended to see the thing ended, and
know what old Thomas had found after all.
Well, when I got there, at the top of the stair, I
turned round to see where Adam might be; but,
thank ye, no Adam had ventured with me!
However, I heard where old Thomas Baffin was
chuckling and laughing, and "Come up," says
he, "and then you shall see what this riot and
rout has been all about!" So through his own
chamber, I onward did clamber, and out on the
leads saw a cluster of heads, and 'mong them
old Thomas's face with a grin of the merriest

meaning that ever was seen. "Oh master,"
says he, "come up here to me, and I'll shew
you a sight worth another such fright!" Well,
I went up, and what do you think I should find?
Old Growler and Vixen the cat, and the raven
that's blind; and betwixt them a great big
shin-bone of a horse, which they jumbled about
without any remorse—and gnawed at and clawed
at, and fought for like mad; and a terrible
battle, no doubt, they had had!

But ere I have done I must tell you the fun
we had in expelling the ghost from the dwelling.
Down stairs in a flurry, we drove hurry-scurry,
with a "Whist!" and a "Hey!" old Vixen
away; then Growler went next, half ashamed and
perplexed, with his great dangling tail like a
torn wind-mill sail, and after him blundering the
big bone went thundering—knock—knock down
the stairs at a terrible rate, and gave our friend
Adam a bump on the pate; but ere he had time
for a grunt or a groan, flap, flap went the blind
raven over the bone, right into the kitchen both
croaking and screeching!

Next after the three came down Thomas and
me; very great with our glory, as you may con-
ceive. So here ends my story, and I take my

leave ; and the sooner, the better, you send me
a letter.

So Peter, goodbye,
You know well that I
Am your friend, as of old,
MATTHEW NOGGINS of Wold.

June, 1864.

THE THREE WISHES.

F

THE THREE WISHES.

"WELL," said George, "if I might choose, I'd
rather be Julius Cæsar than any man that ever
lived! He was a fine fellow, he conquered all
the then-known world—from the pyramids of
Egypt to the island of Thule—from the most
remote provinces of Asia Minor to the western
shores of the Peninsula. In ten years only, he
took eight hundred cities; subdued three
hundred nations; and left above a million of
enemies dead upon his fields of battle! Now he
was a hero! And what a glorious thing it must
have been, after subduing Britons, Gauls,
Germans, and Russians, to return with his
triumphant legions, laden with spoil, and
leading kings captive, a conqueror through the
streets of Rome! I never think of Julius

Cæsar without longing to be a soldier. 'He
came—he saw—he conquered!' How famous
that was. I wish I had lived in his days; or,
better still, I wish there was another world to
conquer, and I were the Julius Cæsar to do it, I
should then indeed be happy. To be master of
the world must be very pleasant."

"Upon my word!" said Charles, "mighty
grand! but if I might choose, I would rather
be Cicero. I'd rather be an orator ten thousand
times than a warrior, though he were Julius
Cæsar himself. Only think, George, when you
came to die, how should you like to have the
blood of a million of men on your conscience?
Depend upon it, it's not such a fine thing to be
a conqueror, after all. But an orator! his *is* a
glorious character indeed. He gains victories
over millions, without shedding one drop of
blood! Now let us match ourselves one against
the other; you a warrior, I an orator—each, let
us suppose, the most accomplished in the world.
What can you do without your legions and your
arms? With ten thousand men at your back,
armed at all points, where, pray, is the wonder
that you take possession of a city or a country,
weakly defended, perhaps, both by men and

means? But place me among savages (provided only I can speak their tongue); give me no arms—no money; nay, even strip me of my clothes, and leave me a defenceless, solitary being among thousands, and what will follow? I will draw tears from the stoniest-hearted among them; they shall give me bread to eat, clothing to wear; they shall build a house to cover me; and, if my ambition extend so far, they shall choose me for their king; and this only by the words of my mouth! Now who, I ask you, is most powerful, you or I?

"You think it was a glorious thing for Julius Cæsar to pass with his captives through the streets of Rome. I think it was glorious, too, for Cicero, when, after having exposed and defeated the horrible conspiracy of Catiline, and driven him from Rome, he was borne by the most honourable men of the city to his house, along streets crowded with thousands of inhabitants, all hailing him 'Father and Saviour of his country!' I wish I could be a Cicero, and you might be a Julius Cæsar and an Alexander the Great for me.

"But come, William," said he, addressing his other brother, "who would you choose to be?

And what arguments can you bring forward in favour of your choice?"

"I," replied William, "would choose to be John Smeaton."

"John Smeaton?" questioned Charles; "and, pray, who in the world was John Smeaton?"

"Bless me!" said George, "not know John Smeaton! He was a cobbler, to be sure, and wrote a penny pamphlet to prove how superior wooden shoes are to Grecian sandals!"

"Not he, indeed!" interrupted William indignantly; "he built the Eddystone Light-house!"

"Oh! yes—yes! to be sure he did. I wonder I should forget it," replied George. "He was a stone-mason, and had the honour of building a wall! Upon my word, sir, yours is a noble ambition! Why Smeaton only did what any man might do."

"Not so, either, my good Julius Cæsar! There are not ten men in England that could have built that light-house as well as Smeaton did. It will stand while the world stands! It is a noble proof of the power and ingenuity of man. It defies the almost omnipotent ocean itself, and the other elements can never affect it.

"And now, George, consider Smeaton's case without your soldiery prejudices. Independently of his work being a master-piece of human skill, its importance will not be lessened by time. Your conquests, most potent Cæsar! are wrested from you in your lifetime, and your successor will hardly thank you for exhausting your country's treasure, and reducing its population for distant empire, which, as soon as you have left it, rises in insurrection, and almost needs re-conquering. Every year, on the contrary, makes that work of Smeaton's additionally valuable; and, as the commerce of the country increases, the importance of that wall, as you are pleased to term it, increases also. There's not a ship that comes into that sea but owes its preservation, in a great measure, to that light-house. Thousands of lives are preserved by it; and when I think of it on a tempestuous night, as I often do, shining out like a star when every other star is hidden, a blessing springs into my heart on the skill of that man who, when the endeavour seemed hopeless, confidently went to work, and succeeded.

"But I'll tell you a story now, about neither

Julius Cæsar, Cicero, nor John Smeaton, and yet which is quite *apropos:*

"There was, once upon a time, a little city that stood by the sea. It was very famous; it had abundance of treasure; twenty thousand soldiers to defend its walls; and orators the most eloquent in the world. You may be sure it could not exist without enemies; its wealth created many, and its pride provoked more. Accordingly, by some Julius Cæsar of those days, it was besieged. Twelve thousand men encamped round its walls, which extended on three sides, and a powerful fleet blockaded the fourth, which lay open to the sea. The inhabitants of this little city felt themselves, of course, amazingly insulted by such an attack, and determined immediately to drive their audacious enemies like chaff before the wind. They accordingly sallied out, but, unfortunately, were driven back, and were obliged to shelter themselves behind their walls. Seven times this occurred, and the enemy had now been seven months encamped there: it was a thing not to be borne, and a council was called in the city.

"'Fight, fight!' cried the orators; 'fight for your homes, for the graves of your fathers, for

the temples of your gods !' But in seven defeats
the soldiers had been reduced to ten thousand,
and the people were less enthusiastic about
fighting than the orators expected. Just then
a poor man came forward, and stepping upon
the rostrum begged to propose three things ;
first, a plan by which the enemy might be
annoyed ; second, a means of supplying the city
with fresh water, of which it began to be much
in need ; third—but scarcely had he named a
third when the impatient orators bade him hold
his peace, and the soldiers thrust him out of the
assembly as a cowardly proser, who thought the
city could be assisted in any way except by the
use of arms. The people seeing him so thrust
forth, directly concluded that he had proposed
some dishonourable measures—perhaps had been
convicted of a design to betray the city ; they
therefore joined the outcry of the soldiers, and
pursued him, with many insults, to his humble
dwelling, which they were ready to burn over
his head.

"Now this poor man, who had never in all
his life wielded a sword, and who had no ambition to do so, and who was but an indifferent
speaker, was, nevertheless, a wise mathe-

matician, and had wonderful skill in every mechanical science then known, which he had the ability, as is common with such men, to apply admirably to every emergency. But he might as well have had no science at all for any respect it won him; and though he was a little chagrined that his well-meant proposition had met no better reception, he shut to his doors, sat down in his house, and turned over his schemes in his head till he was more sure than ever of their success. In the meantime the enemy brought up monstrous battering-rams, crow-feet, balistæ, and all kinds of dreadful engines for the demolishing of the walls, setting fire to the houses, and otherwise distressing the inhabitants. A thousand men were despatched to cut down a neighbouring forest, from the trees of which they began to build immense wooden towers, whence they could sling masses of rock into the city. There was a deafening noise all day and all night without the walls of deadly preparation. The distress of the besieged was now intolerable, and a truce was eagerly desired. A deputation, therefore, of the most honourable citizens, headed by the most eloquent orators, and preceded by a herald bearing a white flag, went to ₊the camp of the enemy. The orators addressed them in the most power- ful, and, as they thought, most soul-touching words; they craved only a truce for seven days; but their words fell like snow-flakes upon a rock—they moved no heart to pity, and the orators were sent back to their city with many marks of ignominy. ' Go back,' said they, ' and our answer shall reach the city before you do.' Accordingly every machine was put in motion. Arrows, hurled by the balistæ, fell into the streets like hail; and ponderous stones, falling upon the buildings, threatened destruction to all. The rest of that day the inhabitants kept within their houses, for there was no security in the streets, nor, it must be confessed, much within doors. The next day, when the enemy a little relaxed their efforts, the people ventured out; but nothing was heard save lamentations and murmurs.

" ' We have no bread,' said the people; ' we are dying of thirst; the little corn that remains, and the few skeleton cattle, are reserved for the soldiers, while we are perishing in the streets! We will open the gates to the enemy, rather than see our children die thus before our eyes !'

" Upon this the orators again came forth. It was now no use mounting the rostrum; the people were sullen, and would not assemble to hear them; they therefore came into the streets, and poured forth their patriotic harangues to the murmuring thousands that stood doggedly together. 'Will ye,' they exclaimed, 'give up the city of your fathers' glory to their bitterest enemies? Speak!—will ye, can ye do it?' And the people held up their pale and famishing children, saying: ' These are our answer—these shall speak for us !'

" Just at this moment, the poor man, filled with compassion for his towns-people, and suffering from want equal to their own, stepped forward. 'Fellow-townsmen,' said he, 'listen! There is no need for us and our children to die of hunger; there is no need for us to deliver up the city. Only do as I say, and we shall have plenty of provision, and may drive our enemies to the four winds.'

" ' What would you have us do ?' asked the people.

" ' Why,' said he, ' for every engine that the enemy brings, bring out one also—defy their battering-rams—disable their crow-feet—sink

a shaft to the river, and have water in plenty!
Give me but seven days, three brave men, and
the means I shall ask, and I will pass through
the enemy's fleet, visit the cities which are
friendly to us, and return with provisions to
stand out the siege yet ten months longer.'

" ' Try him! try him!' said they ; ' we
cannot be worse than we are.'

" There was an instant reaction in favour of
the poor man; all fell to work at his bidding;
every smith's shop rung with the sound of
hammers; carpenters worked all day and all
night, constructing machines which were enig-
mas to them. There was such a hum of business for two whole days, that the enemy could
not imagine what was going forward. In a
short time all was ready. A huge machine,
the height of the walls, was raised, furnished
with a tremendous pair of iron shears, and no
sooner had the enormous crow-foot of the enemy
reared itself to pull down a part of the wall,
than the shears, catching hold of it, snapped it
in two! A roar of applause echoed through
the city, and this first successful effort assured
them all. The poor man at once obtained the
confidence of the city; all the enemy's deadly

machines he counteracted; he set fire to their
immense wooden tower by balls of inflammable
matter, which he flung in at night; and these
exploding suddenly, with horrible crackings
and hissings, terrified the enemy almost out
of their senses, and bursting up into volcano-
like fires, threatened to consume not only the
tower, but the very camp itself. While this
was doing, the poor man and his three colleagues
passed through the fleet in the twilight, in a
small vessel constructed for the purpose, which,
floating on the surface of the water, looked only
like a buoy loosened from its hold. No sooner
were they outside the fleet, than they cut away
one of the enemy's large boats that lay moored
on the shore, and hoisting full sail, by help of a
favourable wind and good rowing, they arrived
by the end of the next day at a friendly city.
There they soon obtained supplies—corn, salted
meat, fresh-killed cattle, and everything of
which they stood in need. A large vessel was
immediately stored and properly manned; her
hull was blackened, so were her masts and sails,
and by good rowing she reached the outside of
the harbour by the next evening. There they
waited till it was quite dark, and then, with

every oar muffled, silently as the fall of night, yet swiftly as a bird, they passed through the midst of the fleet without being detected; and by the next daybreak the vessel lay moored upon the quay of the city.

"That, indeed, was a morning of triumph! Men, women, and children thronged down in thousands. Food was abundant; they all ate and were satisfied. But the extent of the poor man's service was not known when they merely satisfied their hunger; he had induced the friendly city to send yet further supplies, with a fleet, which should not only attack the enemy's ships, but land a body of soldiers, whose object would be to fall suddenly upon the camp in the rear, while the soldiers in the city made a sally on the front. Accordingly, the next day, the sea outside the harbour was covered with ships. The enemy was in great consternation. All fell out as the poor man had foreseen. After very little fighting, the enemy had permission to retire, leaving as hostages three of their principal men, till an amount of treasure was sent in which quite made up the losses of the siege.

"As you may suppose, after this, nobody

thought they could sufficiently honour the poor man ; his deeds were written in the annals of the city, and ever after he was universally called 'the Saviour of his country.'

"And so you see the poor man, by his science and skill, could do more for his city than either soldiers or orators."

"Upon my word," said both the brothers in the same breath, "there's something in it."

THE GRANDMOTHER.

G

THE GRANDMOTHER.

CHILD. And when the house was burned down, grandmother, what did you do then?

GRANDMOTHER. Took shelter in the barn, and and were right thankful that our lives were spared, and that a roof was left to shelter us.

CHILD. But all the furniture was burned, and the beds; and grandfather's leg was broken.

GRANDMOTHER. But there was plenty of good clean straw in the barn, and one neighbour lent us a mattress, and another a blanket; and one brought us a chair, and another a table; many a one spared us a pan or a kettle, a candlestick or an earthen pot, till we could get together two or three things of our own: it was, besides, a special fine season, and even in those misfortunes we had much to be thankful for.

CHILD. But grandfather could not work; and there were five children; and there was the doctor to pay, and the house to build up again ?

GRANDMOTHER. Sure enough! yet, after the first shock of the misfortune, we did better than one might have thought. Thank God! at that time I was not an ailing woman; I was able to work, and everybody was ready to give me a job. Your grandfather, through the blessing of Heaven, soon began to mend, and, saving that he never had the right use of his leg again, was not much worse for his accident. I was soon able to leave him to the care of the three biggest children, and to go out to washing and doing daily work as usual; and many was the time I brought home more than a day's wages, for everybody was kind to us—the farmers' wives often sent us a little bag of meal, or a bit of bacon, or a pitcher of milk; and the butcher sent us a Sunday's dinner for seven weeks—all the time your grandfather was, as one may say, helpless.

CHILD. And then the children had the small-pox ?

GRANDMOTHER. But, by the time they were all down, your grandfather was well enough, though he could not work, to take care of them,

as they lay on the straw he had just risen from.
He was a kind, handy man, and the children all
did well, which was a great mercy, seeing what
a frightful malady it was, and how many died
among the neighbours' children that same
season; then, before winter set in, what with
twenty pounds the squire lent us, and by making
over a bit of common allotment that had come
to us, and with the help of our neighbours, we
got the house raised and the roof on before
the hard weather set in.

CHILD. But it was then, grandmother, that
you got the rheumatism so bad, and that makes
you always so lame?

GRANDMOTHER. Ay, to be sure; we got into the
house before the walls were well dry, and I fell ill
of a rheumatic fever that kept me down fourteen
weeks; but by that time the children were all well
again, and your grandfather could begin to work.

CHILD. But he could not dig as he used to do?

GRANDMOTHER. Why, no; he took to
weaving; and though at first, to be sure,
seeing it was a new trade in his fingers, he could
not get much, yet there's nothing a man cannot
do if he's bent on doing it, nor a woman either;
so, before the spring was over, he got full jour-

neyman's wages; and then, soon after, in a year
or two or so, as it happened, poor old John
Mudge dying, why, he fell into his business as
pat as could be; and weaving was a good trade
then. There was not a farmer's wife in all the
country but had a wheel going, maybe two or
three, and there was a power of yarn spun, both
of linen and woollen, which it was soon thought
nobody could weave into cloth like your grandfather. I'll warrant ye there's bed and table-
linen of his weaving in every decent family
twenty miles round, though it's twenty years
since he died, poor man!—ay, and his weaving
will be remembered through this generation.

CHILD. And that was the way grandfather
came to be a weaver?

GRANDMOTHER. That it was; and it was a
good day's work for him when he first took the
shuttle between his fingers. We got our debts
paid off before three years were over, and then
we were able to lay something by for our children, or maybe, help a poor neighbour. But
now finish the chapter; you left off where the
prophet sat by the brook Cherith, and the
ravens fed him.

CHILD. I will, grandmother.

THE TWO FRIENDS.

•

THE TWO FRIENDS

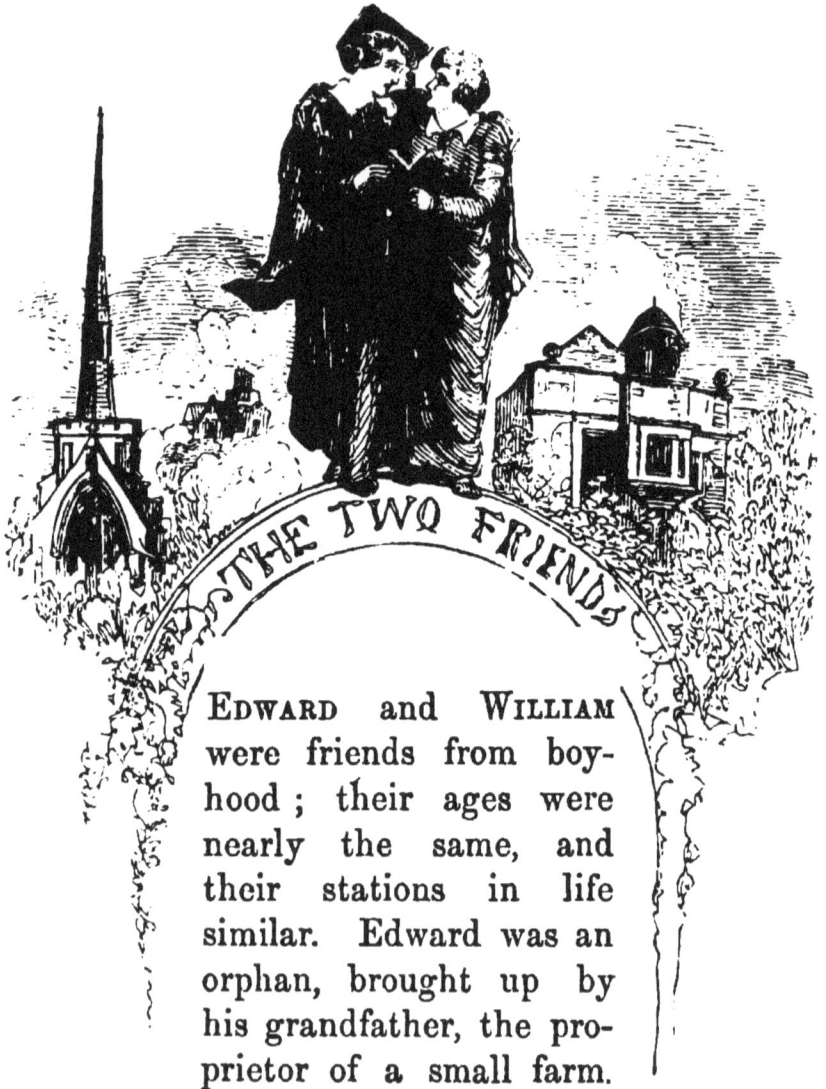

EDWARD and WILLIAM were friends from boyhood; their ages were nearly the same, and their stations in life similar. Edward was an orphan, brought up by his grandfather, the proprietor of a small farm. The father of William was a small farmer also,

a respectable, worthy man, whose only ambition
—and such an ambition was laudable—was to
leave to his son the heritage of a good name.

Both boys were destined by their natural
guardians to fill that station in society to which
they were born ; but it happened, as sometimes
it will happen in such cases, that the boys,
though trained up in hard-working and pains-
taking families—where the labour of the hand
was more thought of than the labour of the
head—were, nevertheless, very bookishly inclined; and as they were both of them *only*
children, their fancies were generally indulged,
and no one took offence that their pence and
sixpences were hoarded up for the purchase of
books, instead of being spent in gingerbread
and marbles. And partly to gratify their own
tastes for learning, and partly to fall in with
the wishes of the village schoolmaster, who
took no little pride and pleasure in his docile
and book-loving pupils, they attended the
grammar-school long after their village con-
temporaries were following the plough. At
fifteen they appeared less likely than ever
voluntarily to lay down Homer and Virgil,
and our English divines and poets, for any

pleasure it was probable they would ever find in growing turnips or selling fat.cattle.

Perhaps this taste for letters might be also stimulated by the grammar-school having in its gift, every five years, a scholarship in one of the universities, and which was awarded to the youthful writer of the best. Greek and Latin theme. The term was about expiring, and one of the two friends was sure of the nomination, there being no other candidate.

It was now Christmas, and the decision took place in March. The themes were in progress, and every thought of both youths seemed to turn itself into good Greek and Latin. Just at this time the father of William suddenly died; and what made the trial doubly afflicting was, that his circumstances had become embarrassed, and the farm must, of necessity, be sold to pay his debts. This was a great sorrow; but, young as William was, his mind was strengthened by knowledge. He turned his philosophy to the best account; he faced his adverse circumstances with manly courage, and with a clear head and an upright heart, assisted in straightening his father's deranged affairs, and in providing that every one's just claim should be satisfied. Yet it was with a heavy heart that he left the comfortable home of former independence, and retired with his drooping mother to a small dwelling with the remnant of their fortune, which was barely sufficient to support her above want.

When William saw his mother's melancholy prospects, he, for a moment, almost lamented that he could not turn his hand to labour; and at times the gloomy thought crossed his mind, that, perhaps, had he been a humble plough-man, he might have saved his father from ruin. But youth is strong, and so is intellect; and the force of a well-stored and active mind buoyed him up, and he felt *that* within him which would not let him despair, nor even murmur; and he knew, besides, that were the scholarship but once won, the way would then be opened to honourable advancement and competency. Vehemently, then, did he bestir himself, and what before was interesting he now pursued with ardour; and what before he had done well, he now did better; for the intellect, like a rich mine, abundantly repays its workers.

Sometimes the idea, almost in the form of a wish, crossed his mind, that Edward, knowing his altered circumstances, might relinquish the field, and thus secure to him what had become so doubly desirable.

It was now the end of January, and, during a hard frost, the two friends met every evening to recreate themselves in skating, an exercise in which both excelled; but William seemed at this time the sport of misfortune, for, as he was performing, almost for the twentieth time, a *chef-d'œuvre* in the exercise, his foot caught a pebble in the ice—he was flung forward to an immense distance with terrible velocity, and in his fall broke his leg. Edward, unconscious of the extent. of the injury, with the assistance of a cottager, conveyed him home insensible. The poor widow's cup of sorrow seemed now full to the brim; and William vainly endeavoured, amid the agony of suffering, to console her. Edward was like a ministering angel; he spoke words of comfortable assurance, and supported his friend in his arms while he underwent the painful operation of the bone being reset.

In a short time the doctor pronounced William out of danger, but he was unable to use the least exertion; even exercise of mind was

forbidden, and days and weeks were now hurry-
ing February into March.

"Alas!" said he, one day, to his friend,
"there is no hope of the scholarship for me;
but why should I regret it, when it only secures
it to you? And yet, for my poor mother's sake,
I cannot resign it even to you without sorrow;
and, dear Edward," he added, his whole countenance kindling up at the idea, "I would have
striven against you like a Dacian gladiator, had
it not pleased Heaven to afflict me thus!"

Edward was a youth of few words, and, after
a pause, he replied, "If your theme is finished
I will copy it for you; mine I finished last
night."

"No," said William, "it is mostly in its first
rough state, and wants a few pages in conclusion; yet you can see it—read it at your leisure;
and, since it is impossible for it to appear, if
any ideas or phrases appear to you good, you
are welcome to them. But I beg your pardon,"
added he, correcting himself, "yours, I doubt
not, is already the best."

Edward did as his friend desired; he took
from William's desk the various sheets of the
unfinished theme. He carried them home with

him, and, without any intention of appropriat-
ing a single word to his own benefit, sat down
to its perusal. He read, and as he read grew
more and more amazed : were these thoughts—
was this language—indeed the composition of a
youth like himself?   ·

He was in the generous ardour of unsophisti-
cated youth, and his heart, too, was devoted to a
noble friendship, and the pure and lofty sentiments of his friend's composition aided the
natural kindness of his heart. It was midnight
when he had finished the half-concluded sentence
which ended the manuscript, and before morning he had drawn· up a statement of his friend's
circumstances, accompanied by the rough copy
of his theme, which he addressed to the heads
of the college ; he also made up his own papers
—not now from any desire or expectation of
obtaining the scholarship, but to prove, as he
said in the letter with which he accompanied
them, how much worthier his friend was than
himself.

All this he did without being aware that he
was performing an act of singular virtue ; but
believing merely that it was the discharge of
his duty. Oh, how beautiful, how heroic is the

high-minded integrity of a young and innocent spirit!

Edward did not even consult his friend the

schoolmaster about what he had done, but took

the packet the next morning to the nearest coach town, and called on his friend William on his return, intending to keep from him also the knowledge of what he had done.

As soon as he entered the door, he saw by the countenance of the widow that her son was worse. He had been so much excited by the conversation of the evening before, that fever had come on; and before the day was over he was in a state of delirium. Edward wept as he stood by his bed and heard his unconscious friend incoherently raving in fragments of his theme; while the widow, heart-struck by this sudden change for the worse, bowed herself like the Hebrew mother, and refused to be comforted.

Many days passed over before William was again calm, and then a melancholy languor followed, which, excepting that it was unaccompanied by alarming symptoms, was almost as distressing to witness. But the doctor gave hopes of speedy renovation as the spring advanced, and, by the help of his good constitution, entire though perhaps slow recovery.

As soon as Edward ceased to be immediately anxious about his friend, he began to be impatient for an answer to his letter; and, in process of time, that answer arrived. What the nature of that answer was any one who had·seen his countenance might have known; and, like a boy as he was, he leaped up in the exultation of his heart, threw the letter to his old grandfather, who sat by in his·quiet decrepitude, thinking that "for sure, the lad·was gone mad!" and then, hardly waiting to hear the overflowings of the old man's joy and astonishment, folded up the letter, and bounded off like a roebuck to his friend's cottage. ·

The widow, like the grandfather, thought at first that Edward had lost his wits; he seized her with an eagerness that almost overwhelmed her, and compelled her to leave her household work and sit down. He related what he had done; and then, from the open letter which he held in his hand, read to her a singularly warm commendation of William's theme, from the four learned heads of the college—who accepted it, imperfect as it was—nominated him to the scholarship—and concluded with a hope, which, to the mother's heart, sounded like a prophecy, that the young man might become a future ornament to the university.

It is impossible to say which was greater— the mother's joy in the praise and success of her son, or her gratitude to his generous friend, who appeared to have sacrificed his prospects to those of his rival. But, while she was pouring out her full-hearted torrent of gratitude, Edward put the letter into her hand, and desired her to read the rest, while he told the good news to William. The letter concluded with great praise from the reverend doctors of what they styled Edward's "generous self-sacrifice;" adding, that in-admiration thereof, as well as in consideration of the merit of his own theme, they nominated him to a similar scholarship, which was also in their gift.

Little more need be added: the two friends took possession of their rooms at the commencement of the next term; and, following up the course of learning and virtue which they had begun in youth, were ornaments to human nature, as well as to the university.

.

FIRESIDE PHILOSOPHY.

FIRESIDE PHILOSOPHY.

"You are but a little fellow, Frank," said the philosophical Philip to his younger brother, "and yet you live in a better and a far more commodious house than a king had formerly. There are ships crossing the sea in every direction, to bring what is useful to you from every part of the earth. The elephant-hunter of Ceylon has dug his traps, and with difficulty and danger taken his prey, that you may have a cup and ball, and play with ivory dominoes. By the shores of the frozen rivers, in the uninhabited regions of the north, hunters have taken the industrious beaver, or the little arctic fox, that you may have a cap or hat made of their fur. The seal-fisher, in the same dreary seas,

wrapped up in skins, has gone on his hazardous
voyage, that you may wear shoes made of fine
and elastic leather.

"In China, they are gathering the tea-leaf
for you. In America, they are planting cotton
for you. In the West India Islands, the poor
negro is toiling in the sun, to provide you with
sugar, and rice, and coffee. In Italy, they are
feeding the silkworms for you. In Saxony,
they are shearing their sheep to make you a
nice warm jacket. In Spain, they have grown
and dried various kinds of fruits, that you may
enjoy a plum-pudding or a mince-pie; and
merchants, coming in ships from the same
country, have brought oranges and nuts for
your eating. And, at this very time, travellers
and voyagers are exploring new and wonderful
regions, that you may know all respecting them,
and benefit by their productions, without you,
yourself, stirring one mile from home.

"In England, steam-engines are spinning and
weaving, and grinding and thumping, and tear-
ing and driving for you; some stationary, like
old-world giants—and others whirling along
railroads by twenties and thirties together like
ponderous dragons, each carriage like a vertebra

of its enormous spine; others are pumping in mines, drawing up with their monstrous arms all metals and minerals that can be useful to you; coal to warm you—and iron and tin, and lead and salt. Fleets are stationed round our happy country to protect and defend it, and that you may sleep and wake without fear of invasion.

"And, little boy as you are, no one could injure you, nor steal you from your parents, without lawyers, judges, nay, even the queen herself, were it necessary, interfering in your behalf. Besides all this, at this very moment men of learning and talent are employed in writing you delightful and instructive books; and printers, engravers, and bookbinders are all working for you, and scheming how they can best please and surprise you. It is a famous thing to live in England—grand old England—in these days!"

"Well, Master Philip," said his sister, who had been listening to his harangue, "may I inquire where you gained all this learning?"

"Not out of my own head, I assure you, Katy; but I heard papa read some remarks, a great deal like what I have said, from the introduction to Dr Arnott's clever book; and, because. I was much pleased with them, I wanted to make Frank feel the same pleasure.'

THE TWO BOYS OF FLORENCE.

THE TWO BOYS OF FLORENCE.

CHARACTERS.

MATTEO LANDO, *the son of* Michel Lando.
LORENZO SCALA, *the son of the* Marquis Scala.
MICHEL LANDO, *the wool-comber, the head of the conspirators.*
The MARQUIS SCALA, *a proud Florentine noble.*
PAOLO, *a Genoese carpenter, uncle to* Matteo.
FATHER BATISTA, *tutor of* Lorenzo.
Boys, Conspirators, Soldiers, &c.

ACT I.

SCENE I.—*Morning. An open space before the Scala Palace.* MATTEO *and three boys throwing with white stones for chestnuts.*

FIRST BOY. I won't make another throw!

MATTEO. Come, don't be angry; you shall have two throws for my one.

FIRST BOY. [*Throwing again.*] There again! It's all cheatery. You got seventeen and I only three. I say you're a cheat!

SECOND BOY. It's my turn now, and I've lost.

THIRD BOY. And so did I. I say he is a cheat and a Ghibeline!

MATTEO. I'm neither! I played fair. If you throw badly, I can't help it!

THIRD BOY. You're a Ghibeline

SECOND BOY. So he is! Down with him!

[*They fall upon him.*

STRANGE BOY. Heyday, what's up now?

ALL. Only beating a Ghibeline.

STRANGE BOY. That's right, down with him.

LORENZO SCALA. [*Opening a gate in the wall*] How now, fellows! Four against one! Shame on ye for a cowardly crew.

THE FOUR. Down with the Scala, he is a Ghibeline too!

LORENZO. [*Throwing off his cloak.*] Touch me if you dare! [*To* MATTEO.] Stand by me, boy, and I'll stand by you. [*They fight, and the four boys are driven off.*] And now, boy, who are you, and what? Guelph or Ghibeline? If Ghibeline, stand to it.

[*He puts himself in an attitude of defence.*

MATTEO. Nay, noble sir, we 'll never fight, I 'm a Guelph, and the son of a Guelph; my father is Michel Lando, the wool-comber, as brave and as honest a man as any in Florence And now, gracious sir, accept my humble thanks; you are a noble young gentleman!

FATHER BATISTA. My lord! my lord! what in the name of the seven angels are you doing?

[*He pulls him in and shuts the gate violently.*

MATTEO. He has left his cloak. Shall I knock, and give it to the porter? No, if that grim monk sees me, he will suspect me of treason, and will say I have polluted the cloak by touching it. I will find some means of delivering it to that noble young lord myself, for I have not half thanked him. He is a fine youth—what an eye!—what a manly carriage!—what a bravo generous spirit! I will give him the cloak myself, and carry with it some little token of my gratitude. Let me see—what can I give him? Oh, I know—I don't believe he ever saw such a thing. But stay—before I go I must roll up this fine purple cloak, and keep it out of sight, or I shall have a mob at my heels and be beaten for a Ghibeline.

[*He rolls up the cloak, and runs off.*

SCENE II.—*A Carpenter's shop.* PAOLO *at work.*

PAOLO. [*Wiping his forehead with his apron.*] What a stupid city is this Florence! A·man may well be thirsty—not a drop of water but what is in that little river Arno! Why, the air's as hot as fire—no sea-breeze like that at Genoa! But here comes my nephew. Well, Matteo, what do you want?

MATTEO. [*With a little ship in his hand.*] I want you to help me with this ship—will you, uncle? I began it six months ago when I was with you at Genoa.

PAOLO. Finish it, and welcome, yourself; but you will get no help from me to-day, I promise you.

MATTEO. Why not, dear uncle, are you busy?

PAOLO. Why, no, not busy exactly, but I'm killed with heat; I don't like Florence.

MATTEO. Well but, uncle, don't let that vex you. Look at this little ship, good uncle, it only wants masts; just look at it to please me.

PAOLO. Why now, what a gimcracky concern this is! Your rudder won't work; and what a prow! Did you ever see a prow like this? It should be small, you know, to cut the water

like an arrow.! Ay, they've merry times at
Genoa, I warrant, this fine summer weather!
I shall never like Florence, that's certain—
more fool I for leaving Genoa! Now take your
ship, and off with you!

MATTEO. Well but, uncle, will you lend me
your tools then, and I'll finish it. I did it all
myself.

PAOLO. And pretty work you've made of it!
But if I must do it, why I must—and I may as
well do it at first as at last. But why do you
want it just now?

MATTEO. To tell you the truth, uncle, I'm
going to give it away.

PAOLO. Give it away! and that's the value
you set on my work, is it? And pray, to whom
are you going to give it?

MATTEO. Why—it's to nobody in particular—
to nobody that you know, dear uncle, only to
the Marquis Scala's son.

PAOLO. Only to the Marquis Scala's son! No
no, sir: if you keep company with nobles, it's
below you to ask favours of a poor carpenter.
Take your ship, I'm not going to spend my
time in making presents for people who will
trample on me in return!

I

MATTEO. Nay, uncle, nay, you're altogether mistaken—Lorenzo Scala will trample on no man! You see this black eye, you see this gash on my arm too, they were given me by my equals, because they said I was a Ghibeline, and young Scala stepped in, threw off his cloak, rescued me, fought himself against four, and drove them off. They would have killed me, uncle, if he hadn't come!

PAOLO. Indeed! That's more than I should have looked for, and I'll take it as a sign that the generation is mending. And so you want to repay him—well, that's only right—doing as you would be done by, as Father Nicolo says. Now for the ship, and let's see what we can make of it. Oh, oh, I see it'll do; a little trimming here, and trimming there, and I'll make it as pretty a thing as ever left Genoa.

MATTEO. Thank you, dear uncle, thank you a thousand times—but let me say one thing, I don't think I can repay him by giving him this ship. I only want to shew that a poor boy can be grateful.

PAOLO. Well, well, that's the same thing, isn't it? But come, my tools are at home—so don't stand prating there.   [*They go out.*

SCENE III.—*Afternoon. The garden of the Scala Palace.* MATTEO *and* LORENZO *before the basin of a fountain, the cloak lying beside them.*

LORENZO. [*Holding the ship in his hand.*] And so you have brought me this beautiful ship! and you say you mean to give it to me, you are very good indeed! But how did you get in? Was the door in the wall open?

MATTEO. No, but I am known to the porter; he often comes to my father's.

LORENZO. And you say this is like a real ship; you know I have never been to Genoa nor Naples. And these are the masts, and these the sails?

MATTEO. Yes, noble sir, and I call it the *Scala,* in honour of you. Ah, if you had but seen, as I have, at Genoa, a whole fleet of their grand merchant-ships going out, and seen thousands of people out on the quay, and heard them shout till the very sky rang again, you would never forget it as long as you lived!

LORENZO. Have you another ship like this?

MATTEO. No. Why?

LORENZO. Because you must be sorry to part

with it; I'm sure I should. I wish I could give *you* something. I'll give you this sword.

MATTEO. No, no, thank you! You did enough for me this morning. No, I'll not take your sword; you know I could not wear it—plebeians cannot wear swords. But I hope you'll live to be a man, and then you'll treat the poor kindly; and when you see the poor oppressed, help them as you helped me this morning!

LORENZO. By the faith of a nobleman, I will! But why do you smile?

MATTEO. Because I know there are many who would say that was a bad pledge.

LORENZO. Do people doubt that? Nay, boy, I tell you solemnly, that if I make a promise, I'll die sooner than break it! But will this ship sail?

MATTEO. To be sure it will! Try it in this basin; you will find it as good a sailer as ever left Genoa. I'll push it where the water is roughest.

LORENZO. No, let me! Huzza, little ship! Huzza! Success to the *Scala!* Is that the way they shouted?

MATTEO. Yes, but a thousand times louder; and waved their caps, and shouted thus.

[*He shouts*—LORENZO *joins him.*

THE MARQUIS SCALA. [*Suddenly coming forward.*] And pray what riot is this? Lorenzo, what low companion have you chosen? Have you so far forgotten the dignity of our house as to bring a fellow like this into our palace garden?

LORENZO. Father, he's a noble-hearted boy, the son of an honest man, and a true Guelph, father!

THE MARQUIS. [*To Matteo.*] How dared you, audacious villain, enter this place? The very air is contaminated with your breath! Out with you!

LORENZO. Be gentle with him, father, he is a generous youth; he gave me this ship, father.

THE MARQUIS. And have you, mean-spirited boy, taken a present at the hand of a plebeian? Out of my sight, ignoble as you are!

[*He offers to strike him.*

MATTEO. My lord, you shall not strike him!

THE MARQUIS. Base son of the earth, dare you defy me? [*He thrusts him out of the gate, and throws the ship after him.*] And now, craven-spirited boy, begone, lest I forget that you are my son!

[LORENZO *goes hastily, his father slowly follows.*

ACT II.

Scene I. *A wool-comber's shop.* Michel Lando, *a stout-built, well-looking man, at work;* Matteo *at work also; three of the* Conspirators *come in.*

1st Conspirator. Good-morrow, friend; at work, as usual.

Michel Lando. To be sure ; sitting still wins no man's bread. But I think I know your errand.

2d Conspirator. If you do not, you soon will. We are come to tell you, Lando, that we don't choose to stir unless you'll take the management of affairs, as usual.

Michel Lando. I say now, what I said then. Be determined as you will, but be moderate. Let not plunder and revenge be the only end for which we strive. Our rights, as citizens and as men, are what we contend for ; let our friends remember this, and I shall not again desert you.

2d Conspirator. But, Lando, we have agreed to obey you.

Michel Lando. Let the nobles enjoy their palaces and their treasures—let the present privileged classes partake in the government of the city, and only such be incapable of holding offices in it who have been, or shall be, · guilty of a crime. Let us contend like men for our rights, but let us be temperate. If you will swear to these restrictions, I will go with you; and, hand and heart, there shall be no truer man than Michel Lando!

3D CONSPIRATOR. We have agreed to obey you in all things. But you must go with us, Michel—we can do nothing without you.

MICHEL LANDO. Let me finish this wool, and then I will attend to you. In the meantime, what has been done since I left?

1ST CONSPIRATOR. Ay, Michel, you bore with them like a saint. You heard what I said; says I, of all the men——

MICHEL LANDO. Yes, good friend, I heard it; but never mind it now. The soldiers had joined us to a man; so had the households of the nobles: the question was, whether the shoe-makers and leather-dressers would join us, or make a party of their own.

2D CONSPIRATOR. They have sworn to join us, if you take the lead, as usual, and then all will be ready. We've chains prepared for the end of every street; arms for every man;

torches ready for lighting; many hundred tons
of stones to defend ourselves with, in case the
nobles are rash enough to face us. The palaces
of the Malatesti, the Ubaldi, and the Scala, are
to be set fire to—all is ready—you know you
consented to that.

MICHEL LANDO. Yes, because some sacrifice of
this kind is necessary to terrify the proud nobles
into reason, and because from the tyranny of
these houses the people have suffered most.
You understand me—no man but myself must
give orders to-night—and my orders shall be
implicitly obeyed.

ALL. They shall, Michel. We understand
you. But come, your work is finished, and our
friends will be impatient.

MICHEL LANDO. I am ready.

[*They all go out.*

MATTEO. They never thought about me—well,
I am possessed of their secret, but I will not
betray it. I will, however, save the life of
Lorenzo. This will be a terrible night! and
poor Lorenzo is doomed to perish for the tyranny
of his proud father: but he shall not—I will
save him! They said the households of the
nobles had joined them—ha!—this accounts

for the porter's intimacy with my father. Yes, yes, I see it all now—but I will save Lorenzo!

[*He goes out.*

SCENE II. *Twilight.* MATTEO, *with great precaution and anxiety, looking out from a pavilion in the garden of the Scala Palace.*

MATTEO. I wish he would come! I feel as if I were just by the jaws of a lion! But hush —here he is. [*Enter* LORENZO.

LORENZO. Why are you here—and why have you sent for me? Oh, do not stay; if my father find you, he will kill you. And Father Batista is as bad! But what is it you want with me?

MATTEO. There is no time for explanation, you must come with me: if you would be living by this time to-morrow, you must come with me. Put on this cloak of mine, that you may not be known; nay, are you afraid of touching it—it will not pollute you!

LORENZO. No, I am not afraid of touching it; but why must I go with you—and whither?

MATTEO. The whole city is in insurrection against the nobles—your palace will be burned this night, and you must perish unless you fly with me.—I can save your life!

LORENZO. What, and let my father perish? No, I cannot—I cannot leave my father; if you can save him too, your offer will be noble: but·I cannot leave my father!·-

MATTEO. But if I save him, he must see me —and you said he would kill me if he saw me. Besides—and yet, noble Lorenzo, for your sake, I will save him.

LORENZO. Now, that's a fine fellow!

MATTEO. Run hastily and prepare your father. Tell him I, the poor boy whom he thrust forth this morning, must see him.

LORENZO. I will. If he be calm, I will bring you before him; if not, I will even take my chance with him—he is my father! And now, the good saints be with you, boy, if we never meet again.   [*Lorenzo goes out.*

SCENE III. *The Saloon of the Palace. The* MARQUIS *seated in a large chair.* LORENZO *leads in* MATTEO.

THE MARQUIS. [*After eyeing* MATTEO *very sternly*]. And you bring report of an insurrection in the city? Our lives, it seems, are

threatened—our palaces to be burned—we are
to die like· slaves, and all this without being
able to make one effort to save ourselves! Do
not think to impose upon us by your idle
threats and false alarms—you shall not go
unpunished!   •
. MATTEO. Do not talk of idle threats, my lord
—for these threats of yours are such ; pardon
me that I speak plain—your life, and the life of
many another noble of Florence, is even now in
danger! ·

THE MARQUIS. Young man, you seem to have
forgotten that nobles·can command both servants
and soldiers !

MATTEO. My lord, it is impossible now; both
your soldiers and servants have joined the conspiracy against you. There is no one in this
palace but looks forward impatiently to the
burning and plundering of it to-night—there
is no one who would not willingly take my life,
because I have sought to save yours! You are
encompassed on all sides—fagots, my lord, lie
under your feet, ready to be kindled—the
tapestry conceals combustibles.
[*He lifts the tapestry, and shews fagots and
straw.*]

THE MARQUIS. Gracious heavens, we are betrayed !

MATTEO. Trust in me, my lord, and you shall be safe !

THE MARQUIS. What can have induced *you* to volunteer so much in our service ?

MATTEO. Gratitude, my lord, to this young nobleman, your son. He rescued me from danger : I owe him more than my service can pay : he was the first nobleman that I have seen do a noble action.

THE MARQUIS. Young man, your services shall be rewarded.

LORENZO. Dear father, let us fly ! Let us confide in this generous youth—why do you hesitate ?

MATTEO. In two hours the attempt will be vain ! I will go and provide means for securing your flight. Pack up as speedily and secretly as possible your most portable treasure ; but whatever is done, let it be done unknown to your servants. If they suspect your flight, all is lost. I will return in half an hour ; but let me find you in the pavilion.   [*He goes.*

SCENE IV. *Two hours before midnight. The Pavilion. Enter* MATTEO, *with a large bundle, a basket, and a dark lantern; the* MARQUIS *and* LORENZO, *with two caskets, enter directly afterwards.*

MATTEO. [*Opening the bundle.*] These clothes you must put on. Pardon them, my lord, they are very humble, but in them your life will be secure. This cloak you must throw over all, and this hood, too, if you please. You must personate my aunt, who lives out of Florence, and regularly brings to the city eggs and poultry; she has come in this day: and you, being taken for Michel Lando's sister, will be safe. She has a son, too, about the age of yours: the night is dark, my lord, and we shall not be detected. Your treasure I will put in this basket, and carry for you.

THE MARQUIS. And must I, indeed, submit to this mummery?

MATTEO. Call it not mummery, my lord— your life, and the life of your son, depend upon it. Trust to me, noble sir, and you shall be safe.

[*They put on the disguises.* MATTEO *darkens*

the lantern, takes up the basket, and goes out—
they follow.]

MATTEO. This way, my lord ; we must escape
by the garden wall, or your servants will discover
us.   [*They all go out.*

SCENE V. *Street.   Crowds of men collected together.   A
chain drawn across the street, guarded by soldiers.   Enter
MATTEO, the MARQUIS, and LORENZO.*

SOLDIER. Who comes here ? Ay, a woman
at this time of night ! Good lady, haven't
you heard that no woman is to stir out on the
penalty of Lando's displeasure ?

MAN. [*Rushing forward*]. 'Tis a man in
disguise !

SECOND MAN. Stop him ! Pull off madam's
hood !

MATTEO. Townsmen ! Do you know me ?

MAN. Ay, sure. Michel Lando's son.

MATTEO. Well, then, let us pass !

THIRD MAN. It is Lando's sister—I saw her
come in this morning.

MATTEO. Let us pass—good people.

            [THE SOLDIERS *undo the chain.*

MAN. The order about the women was Lando's

own. One would think he should not have been
the first to break it!

[*The midnight bell tolls. A sound like thunder
bursts forth, and the darkness becomes suddenly
illuminated. The crowd thickens.*]

MAN. Hurrah!—hurrah! Now dawns a new
day for Florence! Down with the Malatesti!
—down with the Scala!

THE MARQUIS. It, indeed, was too true!
Unfortunate Florence!

MAN. What voice was that! Who bewails
Florence?

MATTEO. Silence, my lord, or we are undone!

ANOTHER MAN. That's the woman! Stop her
—she bewails Florence!

ANOTHER MAN. 'Tis a noble in disguise—stop
him! Bring hither a torch!

[*The people gather about the* MARQUIS, *and lay
hands upon him.*]

MATTEO. Pray you, good people, peace! I am
Michel Lando's son; let us pass, I beseech you!
Can you not trust the son of Michel Lando?

MAN. Michel Lando's son shall go free!—for
shame, towns-people!

ANOTHER MAN. Who's for the plunder of the
Scala palace!

MATTEO. Let us on—let us on!

MAN. The Ubaldi palace is in flames—come! come!

[MATTEO, *the* MARQUIS, *and* LORENZO *go forward.*]

SCENE VI. *A bowshot without the gate of Florence.* MATTEO *gives the basket to the* MARQUIS, *and taking from under his coat the dark lantern, puts it into* LORENZO's *hand.*

MATTEO. Now, my lord, you are safe. There's many a noble life will be lost this night in Florence—but you are safe!

THE MARQUIS. Unfortunate Florence!

MATTEO. [*To* LORENZO, *aside*]. God bless you! remember the promise you made me this morning—always to take the part of the poor when you see them wronged.

LORENZO. I will! And by the faith of a true nobleman, most worthy Matteo, we will reward thee for this!—will we not, father?

THE·MARQUIS. My son, we will! Give me thy hand, young man; thou hast taught me one thing, for which I thank thee—thou hast taught me that there is virtue among the poor! Good-night!

MATTEO. My lord, good-night! Noble Lorenzo, good-night! · [*They separate.*

SUBJECT OF THE PRECEDING DRAMA.

IN the fourteenth century, Florence was governed in.a singular manner: not by a king, nor a senate, but by twelve men, chosen from the trades and professions of the city—the lawyers, the apothecaries, the druggists, the linen-drapers, &c., excluding the lower class of tradesmen, as shoemakers, wool-combers, carpenters and such-like, from any participation in the government. This, of course, led to continual contention between the people and the privileged parts of the community, while, at the same time, both these lived in perpetual hostility with the nobles, who, notwithstanding their exclusion from any share in the government, contrived to tyrannise over all. Besides these causes of discontent, the whole of Italy was, at that time, divided into two great political parties called the Guelphs and Ghibelines—

J

something like our Whigs and Tories. All these causes concurring occasioned more animosity, family feuds, and bloodshed than can be conceived, except by those who know anything of the histories of those times.

The character of Michael Lando, the wool-comber, is known to the readers of Florentine history. Though a conspirator, he was a virtuous man, and distinguished himself in the insurrection which makes part of the subject of the preceding little drama, by his wisdom and moderation.

BARZILLAI BUNKER AND

THE THIEF.

BARZILLAI BUNKER AND
THE THIEF.

THERE was one Barzillai Bunker, a member of the Society of Friends, residing near New Concord, in the back-settlements of New Jersey. He was of wonderfully staid demeanour, and of such inflexible features, that you might have doubted if he could smile; assuredly a laugh was beyond the power of his muscles: yet Barzillai had a spice of humour in his composition, and, in a quiet way, enjoyed a joke as much as any man.

Barzillai was a farmer, and had a small location a short distance from the settlement of New Concord. It was in January, or, as Friends call it, the first month in the year 1795; and

near Barzillai's abode lived one Jonas Familyman, a lazy good-for-nothing fellow, who had
taken a small tract of land, which he managed
much as the sluggard managed his garden in
the days of good king Solomon. The cattle of
Jonas, as may be imagined, were not overwell
supplied with winter fodder; and, as he was too
improvident to have wherewithal to barter, and
money was out of the question, after the wolves
had devoured his three sheep, there seemed no
other way to him of keeping life in the bodies
of his three cows, than by making free with the
rich haystacks of his flourishing neighbour Barzillai Bunker. Barzillai, who would have missed
a straw had it been taken, soon saw that other
than his own people cut the rick, night after
night. But Barzillai, if he were quicker sighted
than most men, was also less communicative,
and not one word did he say of his suspicions.

All this time, however, he was thinking to
himself what he should do, and accordingly,
having made up his mind, on sixth-day, or as it
is commonly called, Friday, night, he took a
dark lantern in his hand and seated himself
under one of his ricks. Here he had not been
long stationed before he perceived his neighbour

Jonas quietly steal up, seat himself in a partly-cut rick, and ply the cutting-knife with tenfold the agility he commonly used, on either ordinary or extraordinary occasions. Barzillai was glad to see that his neighbour had the proper use of his arms, and could make them move when it suited his purpose.

In a short time Jonas had released a handsome truss from the stack, and heaving it upon his shoulders, quietly, and securely, as he thought, marched off with his plunder, little thinking, poor man, that Barzillai was tracking his heels all the time. A merry thought meanwhile was in Barzillai's head, and he advanced upon him until they came to a lonesome piece of unreclaimed swamp which Jonas had to pass. Barzillai was concealed from sight by the burden which poor Jonas carried, and just as they were at the entrance of the frozen swamp, he took the candle from the lantern and set fire to the hay on either side, and then, extinguishing his light, slipped aside to see what would come of it. On Jonas went a few paces, unconscious of the growing conflagration at his back, till it suddenly burst forth into a wild blaze and seemed to envelop him in fire. Down, in a

moment, went the blazing mass, and the poor
thief stood revealed by the clear flame through

the darkness. In an agony of sudden horror
his hands were extended wildly forward; his
hair lifted his fragment of a hat from his head,
and then, after a cry, between a scream and a

groan, he darted forward like a maniac, not daring to look behind him till he was totally lost in the blackness of the night.

After witnessing this spectacle, Barzillai went quietly home to his bed. The place was so lonesome, and inhabitants so few, that there was no probability of the circumstance having been witnessed, and he said not a word to any of his household of what he had done or of what he had discovered.

The next morning, poor Jonas, pale, and with his lean melancholy figure looking yet more woe-begone, came to the house of Barzillai.

" Oh ! " he exclaimed, when he found himself alone with his neighbour in his comfortable parlour, " I have been a wicked wretch, I have been a thief—good Mr Bunker, forgive me ! " and saying that, he fell upon his knees before him.

" What is it thou hast done, friend? what is it thou wouldst have of me?" asked Barzillai with great serenity.

" Oh, worthy, good Mr Bunker," cried Jonas, " the vengeance of the Almighty has pursued me. I have robbed your stacks time after time, but last night fire from heaven consumed

my plunder, and it is of the Lord's mercy that
I am spared ! "

"Rise, my friend," said Barzillai, "thine is a
strange confession."

"It is to you," cried Jonas, still on his knees,
"that I must make confession, and from you I
must obtain .pardon, before I can implore for-
giveness of Heaven! I have been a sinner all
my days, Mr Bunker, but this Providence of
Mercy has redeemed me, and from last night I
shall be an altered man !"

All sense of joke was gone from the mind of
honest Barzillai, and he, too, like the poor peni-
tent, was humbled by the sense of the Almighty's
influence, which had thus made him an instrument to reclaim his poor erring brother. Barzillai leaned against the rude mantel-piece of his
parlour, and wept; and then taking poor Jonas
by the hand, seated him beside him, freely
forgave him for what he had done, and began
such a conversation with him as strengthened
all his good resolutions.

Jonas and Barzillai wept together; it was
like the repentant prodigal coming back to his
father's house: and Barzillai lived to witness
the rich and abundant fruits of the poor man's

penitence, in the happy change which took place, not only in his outward circumstances, but in his whole conduct. Of course he kept secret his own share in the event of the night; he had neither wife nor child to communicate it to, and he learned to love the repentant Jonas too well to hint a word to his discredit. The whole circumstance never would have transpired had he not accidentally related it to an old Friend in England, during one of his religious visits to that country.

Barzillai has long been dead, but the descendants of Jonas Familyman are a numerous and flourishing colony, in and about New Concord.

A BRIEF MEMOIR OF

CONSTANTINE AND GIOVANNI.

A BRIEF MEMOIR OF

CONSTANTINE AND GIOVANNI.

BY THEIR SISTER.

————— near Bath, 1829.

WE were three orphans, Constantine, Giovanni,
and myself. There was two years' difference in
all our ages ; and Giovanni, the youngest, was
only a year old when my mother died—my
father had then been dead about six months.
He was a painter, a man of fine imagination ;
and the few pictures he left at his death are
now fully estimated by the public. Hundreds
of pounds are paid eagerly for one of his female
heads ; and one of his landscapes sells for more
than he ever obtained during his lifetime for all
the paintings he sold.

My mother was a young Florentine lady, whom my father had married while pursuing his studies in Italy. I remember her; a vision of grace—tender and kind: but my recollection of the expression of her countenance and the beauty of her features has been assisted by her portrait painted by my father; which, with his own, was the only one reserved, when, after his death, the rest of the pictures were sold. They were unframed, and hung in our little room, and with them constantly before my eyes, I seem never to have forgotten my parents. My mother's countenance is one of the tenderest and most feminine beauty—long, rich, dark hair, a high forehead, pure as the finest marble, features well defined, but extremely delicate, and perhaps most striking from an expression of deep melancholy and thought. It was in itself a study, and might have passed as such, had it not been known as a portrait. No wonder was it that my father loved her! Hers was the face from which he drew his female countenances, and they had all the spirituality and tenderness so conspicuous in hers. Besides her beauty she possessed a rare and glorious gift—the gift of music in the highest perfection; and full of the

intense poetry of her own land, she had, like a
few of her countrymen, the power of improvisa-
tion. I remember her singing in a low tone,
strains so sweet, that, young as I was, I felt as
it were chained to the spot. Constantine remembered her well: he said she most frequently
sang when my father painted; he said too,
that she very rarely sang except in her native
tongue; which, indeed, my father and she so
commonly used, that Constantine and myself
spoke it more fluently than English. With such
a woman, possessing at the same time the
kindest affections and most amiable dispositions,
could my father be other than happy? They
lived in a country beautiful as their own imaginations, and each indulging their favourite tastes,
and surrounded by us, whom they most tenderly
loved, their lives passed on, if not splendidly, at
least happily. From a few circumstances, however, which Constantine could remember, I fear
they knew what it was to be poor. But the
sorrows of poverty we never experienced: we
lived amidst affection, in the free exercise of our
limbs in the open air. Green hills, sweet clear
waters, beautiful flowers and butterflies—these
fill the recollection of those early years.

K

But my father died. I know nothing of the particulars of his illness; I only remember my mother's utter distress—her weeping for days—the funeral, a sad but incomprehensible scene—and a silence and gloom in our house from which we fled to our favourite resorts in the fields.

What my mother's family was I did not at that time know; we were too young to be made confidants in these things; but I have often wondered she did not return to Italy. My father had no near connections; none to whom she could fly, either for comfort or assistance. She was a widow in a strange land!

Soon after my father's death, her health began to droop; a deep melancholy settled on her spirits, but the sweetness of her character won the love and kind attentions of all around her—poor and uneducated though they were. Fortunately, too, at this time she became known to the pastor of the mountain district in which we resided; a humble, kind, and most excellent man. Through his agency she was enabled to sell a few pictures which remained at very considerable prices; for their value, on account of the death of the artist, was greatly increased.

By this means she became possessed of a little independence, which, while it raised her above want, tended but in a small degree to remove her anxieties on our account. To the good man she unburdened her heart. He voluntarily took upon himself the character of a parent towards us—which character he faithfully sustained to the last day of his life.

Six months after my father's death, as I said before, we lost our beloved mother. Alas! then we first knew sorrow. In six months the understanding of a child makes great advance; and death, which in the first instance may be little felt, is an event too awful not to become deeply impressive by its repetition. Thus insensible perhaps, as we might be, to the loss of my father, we deeply mourned now—Constantine and myself at least, we knew that we were orphans—that most melancholy of all conditions. God, however, had provided a protector in the excellent man who had been as a father also to our poor mother, and by whom she had indeed been regarded as a daughter.

After my mother's death, our kind friend arranged our little affairs. Our small property was invested advantageously, and produced a sum, though abundant for our maintenance, totally inadequate to procure us an education better than could be obtained in our humble district; but this was a loss of less importance, since we were every day with our pastor. Kind, worthy old man, how more than parental was his care over us! He was a widower, and his had been a childless house till he adopted us; then he bestowed upon us all the love of his affectionate heart. He taught us all that we knew; he studied our tastes, and cultivated our understandings, and gave us a self-dependence of character, which, circumstanced as we were, was of great service to us in after life. And all this was done by a man nearly seventy years of age, for the children of strangers! He read with us, walked with us, partook of our sports; and we in return venerated, nay, almost adored him. So passed nine years of our life.

Constantine was the noblest-looking boy I ever saw, and his spirit accorded with his person—generous, kind-hearted, and daring, no adventure was too perilous for him; he was the companion of the shepherds in their mountain rounds; he had climbed every cliff, swam across every lake, and knew every glen and lonely dwelling in our wild and sequestered country. He was a favourite with all; for he was manly, clever, and full of humour and wit. Giovanni was formed in a different mould: he strongly resembled my mother; had the same features, the same sweet, sad expression of countenance. He was delicate, too, in constitution, and was incapable of partaking the boisterous sports and daring adventures of his brother. So framed and so constituted, he was much less generally a favourite than Constantine. The truth was, there were none, save our pastor, who could understand and appreciate him; he was too full of natural refinement for common minds, and he shrunk from their coarse manners—nay, from their rude kindness—with a morbid delicacy which was often mistaken for pride, and sometimes worse, for ingratitude. With his personal resemblance to my mother, he also inherited her talent for music. His ear was quick and correct, he seemed to understand it scientifically before he could speak a word; and his dear mother, to the very last, sang to him the sweet and plaintive airs of which he was so fond. Dear child! his whole soul was love and music. Had we lived much in society he would have been, shewn off as a prodigy; as it was, he drew little attention, for our good friend had no taste for music, and consequently but little respect for the art or its professors, and though he indulged Giovanni's talent to the utmost in his power, it was only his childish propensity which he hoped he would outgrow as he approached manhood.

I possessed my father's talent. I cannot recollect the time when I did not attempt to draw every object that pleased me. I made copies of animals, heads, and occasionally designs from my own imagination; nor did I ever hear of any scene, occurrence, or person, which did not immediately present itself to my mind as a picture; these I often struck off at the moment, and the praise they frequently obtained from our partial friend was all the encouragement and reward that I coveted. My early drawings covered, and I doubt not still cover, the walls of the rooms, not only of the parsonage, but of many neighbouring cottages, whose inmates looked upon me as a prodigy of the pictorial art. But enough of myself, I will return to my brothers.

Constantine was now fourteen, and our worthy

friend proposed that he should be brought up to the ministry; entertaining, I believe, the fond hope of his succeeding him in the care of his simple flock. But my brother's earnest wish was to be a soldier. The quiet life of a country pastor had no charms for an active, and not unambitious mind like his; it therefore was with great self-sacrifice that he gave up all his pleasant visions of a most enterprising and conspicuous life. But his studies were scarcely begun when our protector was suddenly snatched from us by death.

He had gone on a visit to a sick man in a neighbouring valley, when, on his return, feeling himself faint, he sat down upon a piece of rock by the wayside. Constantine, who was with him, supported him in his arms; but the hand of death was upon him, of which the good man was conscious.

"I am dying," said he to Constantine; "yet be not alarmed: death has no terrors for me — no pang saving the separation from you, the children of my old age; but God will be a father to you, and will raise you up friends when I am gone!"

Constantine, composed and courageous as he

naturally was, was yet inexpressibly shocked and distressed at the sudden event, and wept bitterly.

"God bless you, my dear son!" faintly exclaimed the excellent old man, feeling Constantine's tears falling upon his hand—"give my love to them at home!"

These were his last words, and the spirit, all purity and love, ascended to its great reward!

Some shepherds happening to pass by shortly afterwards, assisted poor Constantine to convey the body home. Now, indeed, were our sorrows renewed; now again were we orphans!—and not we alone, but the whole district were mourners. A being more beloved never went down to the grave, nor had one of purer life ever existed. His life had been a series of well-doing; he was a sincere, humble Christian, and one of the kindest, most cheerful of human beings: this, indeed, was a part of his Christianity.

A gloomy time succeeded—a long, dreary winter; and when spring came, our minds had not recovered their usual tone. The successor of this excellent man was one of a totally different character. He resided at a great distance, and held this with several other livings. He was a stranger to all his flock, and had no sympathies in common with them. He visited the church twice in the year; at other times, service was performed by the minister of a neighbouring parish, who, having the duties of his own church to attend to also, was only seen once on the Sunday, and, of course, he had no time to bestow upon the people individually. This was a melancholy time, and our forlorn situation excited the kindest sympathy of our poor neighbours, some of whom offered to initiate Constantine in their humble callings, like one of their own children, free of cost. But a high-spirited boy like Constantine could not submit himself to a common handicraft trade; for, poor as we were, we had always an idea that we were of superior birth to those among whom our lot had fallen, and had an undefined belief that we should, in the end, take that place in society which, had our gifted parents lived, their talents would have obtained for us. After Constantine's refusal of the well-intentioned kindness of our neighbours, we were much less objects of compassion than formerly; we were called proud, and the opinion which was entertained of us, but more especially of Constantine, led to an event which made a most painful change in our circumstances, and which I will relate.

Constantine was one day assisting a shepherd in removing his flocks from the hills during a storm, and, in the course of the day, was desired to remain for a short time at a house of refreshment by the wayside. A party of country people, returning from market, were seated within the wooden screen round the fire, and Constantine, unseen by them, found, to his surprise, himself the subject of their discourse. He had no idea till then that he had given such serious affront to his former friends. He was charged with pride, ingratitude, and idleness— with being a burden to the honest people with whom we dwelt. And even the memory of our revered friend was censured for bringing him up with notions so unbefitting his station. Poor Constantine, how little either he or our lost friend deserved these censures!

All this he heard, and his heart rose to his lips, and his cheek flushed with indignation, but he restrained both his anger and his emotion; and when he returned home in the evening, it was with more than his usual vivacity. He related to us all that he had heard; "And now," said he, "I have fixed my plans, and am sure they will succeed."

"What plans, dear Constantine?" asked I, impatiently, for I dreaded his leaving us.

"Since you do not like me to be a soldier," replied he—for I had always opposed his soldierly propensities—"I will be a sailor; and here I will not be opposed. I feel the utmost confidence in myself; I could fancy myself many years older since I have come to this determination. I shall set off for Liverpool to-morrow; and in a few weeks I shall be in the way to make a fortune—a fortune for you also!"

Constantine finished his speech without interruption: had a sudden dumbness fallen upon me, I could not have felt less capable of replying.

"I, too, dear brother," said Giovanni, "will go; I am not the sickly boy they take me for; you shall not run all risks for us; I can do more than you suppose," argued Giovanni, laying his beautiful small hand upon his brother's arm.

"No, no!" said Constantine, with decision; "no, Giovanni, you must stay with Magdeline!

When I am gone, there will be but two to be supported, and there will be plenty. Every sixpence of my share in our little property, from this moment I give up to Magdeline and you!"

I threw myself on his neck—I wept as I had never wept before—I besought him to stay with us—to let us labour all together—to let us submit to anything, rather than be separated: but he was unmoved—his conduct appeared unaccountable to me; he not only appeared firm, but, I thought, stern in rejecting our prayers; and commanded us, as a father might have commanded his children, to drop the subject, and let us finish the evening in joy. "Come, Giovanni," said he, "let us hear some music!"

Giovanni took up the instrument, but he played feebly, and when he raised his voice to sing, sobs choked his utterance. "I am wretched!" said the dear boy, "and I cannot give expression to my feelings. Dear, dear Constantine," continued he, "if you go, I shall never see your face again!" and he wept as if his heart would break. Constantine, too, covered his face with his hand, and we were silent for many minutes.

At length, "Come, come," said he, endea-
vouring to look calm—"come, Giovanni, have
done; this is all folly! And Magdeline," continued he in a gayer tone, "since we cannot
have music, let us see your folio. Have you
anything new to shew me? Will you give me
this?" said he, selecting one from the many
sketches: it was a head of Giovanni.

"Yes," said I, "and this, and this, if you
will only promise not to go to sea!" Alas, I
little thought why he was asking for one; it
was in the fixed resolution of leaving us, and
for a parting token.

The next morning, to our utter consternation, he was gone. He had packed up his
few clothes unknown to any one, and leaving
a few kind words of farewell on a scrap of
paper, which Giovanni found on his pillow,
was many miles distant ere we discovered his
flight.

In three weeks time he wrote to inform us of
what he called his good-fortune. He had made
an engagement with the master of a merchant-
vessel, and was on the point of sailing for the
East Indies. The letter was in a strain of
gaiety, little in accordance with our feelings,

but full of ardent affection, and breathing his own cheerful and sanguine spirit, which always looked forward to the future with confidence. Since then we have heard no tidings of him, saving that the ship in which he sailed arrived safely at her destination. Dear Constantine! would that it had pleased Heaven to reward his virtuous intentions with the success which, according to our human reasoning, they so well merited! Time went on; and though we became in some degree reconciled to his absence, we never ceased mourning for him whom we could consider but as one dead. Still, occasionally we had hope, and we talked over his happy return; the more happy for our uncertainty and fear. But, alas! now my hope is over. I have seen Giovanni laid in his grave, and I feel that I am alone in the world!

But let me proceed with my narrative.   ·

Shortly after Constantine's departure, Giovanni became ill; and though after the lapse of several months he appeared perfectly recovered, I could not avoid remarking, that the resemblance to my mother was stronger than ever— and the resemblance not to her in her strength and health, but in her declining state. This mournful resemblance filled my spirit with inexpressible sadness.

With his weakness, the sweetness of his affectionate nature yet more revealed itself; he leaned on me as on the sole hope of his life ; I was mother, brother, and sister all in one, and my tender affection for him increased more and more. He was dearer because so dependent upon me ; and, weak and feeble as he was, I would not have exchanged him for any living brother in the universe.

I omitted to mention before, that the cottager with whom we resided was the organist of the little church of our hamlet. The organ was a fine instrument for so remote and rarely frequented a place. It had been the gift of a gentleman of great taste and musical talent, who was born and resided many years there ; but who had now removed to a distant part of the kingdom. The organist had been trained under his direction, and would often speak of those times as of a golden age, when people came far and near to hear him perform. " But now," he would say, with a sigh, " the church is deserted, nobody cares for music now a days ! " With the old organist Giovanni was a favourite, and he used, in his most flattering moments, to predict that he should be his successor. The organ was, as may be supposed, Giovanni's delight, and my heart has ached many a time to think that the cause of his delicate health might be attributed to colds he took in practising in the church, even in the severest weather, and from which he could not be deterred, except by extreme indisposition.

When Giovanni was about fourteen, Mr B——, the patron of the parish, after an absence of twenty years, suddenly made his appearance at his native village late one Saturday evening. Whether it was that the good old organist feared to perform again before the critical ear of his patron, or that a sudden indisposition did indeed seize him, I cannot say; but on the following morning he declared himself unable to leave his bed, and lamented that the organ must go unplayed, which he knew would be a great disappointment to Mr B——.

But the organ did not go unplayed upon. "I have practised upon it too often," said Giovanni to me secretly, "not to succeed now." No one but myself knew his design, and at his request I seated myself with him at the instrument, concealing ourselves with the curtains. I saw Mr B—— enter the church, and place himself immediately opposite to the organ, and fixing his eyes upon it, apparently wait with impatience for the performance. Giovanni played with beautiful precision and feeling, and I knew by the gentleman's countenance that he was both surprised and pleased. The sermon was done, a concluding psalm was played, and then I saw by Giovanni's eye his state of mind—he had forgotten time and place, and he poured forth a voluntary, composed at the moment to his own inspired feelings, with which he mingled the clear yet low tones of his sweet voice. The whole congregation was electrified. Simple and uneducated as they were, the expression of that wonderful music touched every soul; and a silence, like that of the grave, succeeded its conclusion—and then a universal whisper, and then a loudly murmured applause; but when they looked for the strange musician, he was not to be found. Short as the effort had been, I saw it had exhausted him, and therefore led him immediately home.

All who knew Giovanni readily conjectured that it was he. Of course Mr B——'s curiosity

was intense; and scarcely stopping to make any
recognitions among his old acquaintance, he
hurried to the organist. The tidings of the
strange performance had already reached him;
and, as during the service he had found himself much better and had left his bed, he went
forth to meet his old patron. "You are come,"
said he, meeting him at the door, "to inquire
who played the organ this morning—you do not
think it was I—you are right—but it was a
youth of whom I, in some sort, may be said to
have had the teaching: he has a fine ear, sir,
and understands the organ as well, pretty near,
as myself?"

"And where is he, and who is he?" asked
Mr B——.

"Poor lad," replied the organist, "he is an
orphan, and as delicate as a crushed flower; he
is the son of ——, a great painter they tell me,
who died under this very roof some fourteen
years ago. But come in, sir, and you shall see
him!"

It was a fortunate day for us; and from that
time forward we never wanted either home or
friends. Mr B—— was one who could understand Giovanni's excitable nature, and sympa-

thise in his feelings—the first person beside his lamented brother, the pastor, and myself, from whom he did not shrink as from a nature totally different to his own.

I will not detail the particulars of the month that followed: in that time. our circumstances had undergone an entire change. We had left, with many regretful feelings, it must be confessed, the cottage among the hills, and its kind and worthy inmates, from whom, in our afflictions, we had ever received the kindest sympathy. We were become the adopted children of a new friend ; we had found a mother in his wife ; and were established, amid abundance and ease, in a quiet mansion near Bath. A new life had opened to us ; but it was too late for Giovanni to enjoy any change, however favourable. The most skilful physicians were consulted on his case, but the more skilful they were, the less hope they gave. Excitement, they all agreed, would kill him ; but it was impossible to keep a nature like his free from it. The stimulus was within ; and things which would not have moved an ordinary mind—a fine sunset, the rich odour of a flower, the pictures that surrounded him, all produced that very state of mind which was death. A dreadful, incessant palpitation of the heart—burning cheeks—a more beautifully brilliant eye, these were the outward and visible signs of his malady ; and it was impossible not to see, from week to week, what havoc it was making in his bodily powers. There was an extraordinary interest excited about him— constant and anxious inquiries after him from hundreds of persons ; for his singular story, which had been made known, and his striking exterior, had attracted much attention ; but, alas ! his days were numbered. Music was now forbidden, and a state of profound rest enjoined as a last hope.

All this time, while his strength was rapidly declining, he could scarcely be made sensible of his danger ; his spirits were generally high, and he took great delight and interest in all that surrounded him ; and had music been permitted him, fatal as it must have been, he would have been perfectly happy. Occasionally, however, a presentiment of death came over him, and his affectionate heart indulged a natural grief in the prospect of leaving us. Still, the hope of meeting again, and conversing with our beloved Constantine, made the prospect of death less

appalling. But why should I prolong so sad a
story ?—He died ! On the last day of his beautiful and innocent life, when all hope for him
was over, he begged for an instrument ; it was
permitted to him, for, said the physician, it
may allay his irritation—and it cannot produce
a worse state than that from which he is now
suffering—alas ! he did not know how frail was
his thread of life—how fatal that indulgence
would be !

There were only Mr and Mrs B—— and
myself with him ; he was reclining on a couch.
When he heard that the use of his instrument
would be permitted him, on condition of his
composing himself for the rest of the day, his
countenance assumed an expression of almost
angelic delight, and with tears in his eyes he
thanked us and promised implicit obedience.
He took the instrument, struck a few feeble
tones—paused a moment, and then, slightly
raising himself, poured forth the whole of his
pent-up feelings in a tide of the most soul-touching music. At length he stopped.

"I can play no more," exclaimed he, and
laying his head upon my shoulder, seemed
gradually to sink into a deep sleep. I believed

he had thus composed himself, when I observed a glance of sorrowful meaning pass between Mr and Mrs B——. I understood it too well!—my beloved brother was no more!

I cannot proceed—the remembrance of that time overcomes me; three years have passed since then; but we never speak of Giovanni without tears.

1830.—My dear brother Constantine still lives!—A letter from him has arrived. What a joyful letter! and yet sorrowful in one respect, since it is addressed both to Giovanni and myself. Colonel Allan, too, of the —— regiment, mentioned in the letter as returning to England, we have seen. He knows Constantine well—what a delight to converse with one that knows him and has seen him but lately!—what a delight, too, to hear the honourable manner in which he speaks of him! Oh, how my heart overflows with gratitude to that good Providence that has sustained him, and preserved him to me!

The following is the brief outline of his history since he left England, as given by Colonel Allan.

He sailed to Calcutta, and thence to New

South Wales, and on his return the vessel was
driven out of her course and wrecked on one of
the Molucca islands, and all the crew perished
excepting five, one of whom was Constantine.
They were detained three years in hard captivity, from which, after a series of adventures
almost as romantic as those of Robinson Crusoe,
they were delivered through the aid of Major
Downing of Madras, who had heard, accidentally,
of a small number of English sailors being
captive in the Moluccas. By this means Major
Downing became acquainted with Constantine,
and presented him with a cadetship in his own
forces. Thus he honourably commenced his
military career. He has since served in two
campaigns up the country, and, according to the
mode of promotion in the Indian service, held,
at the time of his writing, a captain's commission.
All this, it appears, we ought to have known; for
Constantine, his friend says, to his own knowledge, wrote to us—but his letter we never
received. Speaking of himself, my brother
writes thus in the letter now before me:

"I am not the little Constantine you knew
me. I am twenty-one years old; my brown hair
is become black as jet, and I am the colour of

old mahogany; but I am well and happy; the climate agrees with me; I have not been ill for a single day. I have a house of my own; three-and-twenty servants, and a stud of elephants; we live on rice and curry, are as temperate as Brahmins, and yet lead lives like princes. I only want you, my little Magdeline, and Giovanni [would that he had been spared to know these joyful tidings], with his sweet music, and saint-like countenance, to make me perfectly happy. I want you to come here—and I send by my friend, Colonel Allan, about five hundred pounds —this will enable you to do so—Allan will tell you all that is needful to be done, and has the goodness to undertake the management of everything."

My kind friends, Mr and Mrs B——, will not consent to my departure; but instead of myself Constantine will receive tidings both of joy and sorrow; and the time may come, if so Heaven wills it, when we may meet again in England, and talk over the varied events of our singular histories.

MARTHA AND MARY.

MARTHA AND MARY.

I⊤ was when
the persecution
of the people
called Quakers
had, for a short
season, somewhat
abated its rigour,
and they ventured
to attend their re-
ligious assemblies
without fear of in-
jury to their families in the meantime, that Walter Pixley and his
wife, a staid and respectable couple
belonging to that despised community, rode

eleven miles to their county town of Stafford,
to be present at a meeting, at which that
apostle-like young man, Edward Burrough, was
to preach, leaving their little daughter Martha,
under the care of an aged woman, who was, at
that time, their sole female domestic.

Martha was a grave child, though but seven
years of age : her young mind had taken its
tone from both of her parents. She had been
born in a season of persecution, had been
cradled, as it were, in anxiety and sorrow, and
as she grew old enough to comprehend the
circumstances that surrounded her, she saw her
parents constantly filled with apprehension for
the safety of their lives and property. She had
heard them talk over their grievances, spoiling
of goods, the maimings, the whippings, and the
horrible sufferings of their persecuted brethren—
persecuted even to the death ; had heard of
little children enduring, with the stedfastness of
early martyrs, imprisonments and pains which
would overcome even the strong man ; till,
unlike the ordinary child of her years, her
countenance habitually wore a look of gravity,
and her heart bled at the least thought of suffering or sorrow.

Martha's home was in a country place, surrounded by fields—a pleasant, quiet valley, the patrimonial heritage of her father. It was harvest-time, and in the course of the morning the old servant went out with the reapers' dinners, leaving little Martha to amuse herself in her usual quiet way. She had not been long alone, before a beggar-woman presented herself with a young child in her arms. Martha knew that it was her mother's custom to relieve distress in whatever shape it presented itself, and the story the woman told, whether false or true, touched her to the soul; she gave her, therefore, the dinner which had been set aside for herself, and compassionated her in words of the truest sympathy; and when the child in the woman's arms wept, like Pharaoh's daughter, her heart yearned towards it. Strange it may be to all, but so it was (for our story is true), when the beggar-woman saw the affection with which little Martha regarded the child, she proposed to sell it to her, and Martha, innocent of all guile, readily accepted the proposal. All her little hoard of money was produced—the bargain was struck—and the two parted perfectly satisfied with the transaction. The child was beautiful as the Hebrew boy himself, and Martha sat down with it upon her knee, and lavished upon it all the endearing tenderness which her most affectionate nature suggested.

In a short time the child fell asleep, and as she sat gazing upon it, a half-defined fear stole into her mind, that perhaps she had done wrong in taking upon her this charge unknown to her parents—that perhaps they would be displeased. She rose up in haste, and looked from door and window for the beggar-woman ; but neither across the fields, nor down the valley, nor upon the distant highways was she to be seen ; and then, with that sentiment which, from the time of the first error in Paradise, has become a part of our human nature, she was afraid, and thought to hide the child. She made it a comfortable warm bed with a blanket in a large press, and kissing its sleeping eyes, and wishing that she had no fear, she left it to its repose, and began with great anxiety to look out for the return of her parents. To the old domestic she said not one word of what she had done.

After two hours—all which time the child slept soundly—Walter Pixley and his wife returned. The good mother, who was accustomed to help in all the domestic business, employed herself in preparing the early afternoon meal, and Martha sat down with her parents to partake of it. While Walter Pixley and his wife were in the midst of their review of the events of the morning—of Edward Burrough's extraordinary sermon, and of the concourse to whom it was addressed, they were startled by what seemed to them the cry of a child. Martha's heart beat quick, and her sweet face grew suddenly pale; but her parents were not observing her. The good man stopped in the middle of a sentence, and both he and his wife turned their heads towards the part of the house whence the sound proceeded, listened for a second or two, and then, all being again still, without remarking upon what they supposed was fancy, they went on again with their conversation. Again a cry louder and more determined was heard; and again they paused. " Surely," said the wife, " that *is* the voice of a young child."

The critical moment was now come—concealment was no longer possible ; and Martha's affection mastering her fear, as the infant continued to cry, she darted from the table and exclaimed: "Yes, yes, it is my child!" and the next moment was heard audibly soothing her little charge, in the chamber above, with all the tenderness of the fondest mother.

Mrs Pixley was soon at her daughter's side, full of the most inconceivable astonishment, and demanded from her whence the child had come, or how it had been consigned to her charge. Martha related the story with perfect honesty. The old domestic was then summoned, but she knew nothing of the affair. They were not long deliberations that followed. The family could not conscientiously burden themselves with another dependent, and one especially who had no natural claim upon them, in these perilous and anxious times when they could not even insure security for themselves; and besides this, how did they know but this very circumstance might be made, in some way or other, a cause of offence or of persecution, for the world looked with jealous and suspicious eyes upon the poor Quakers. Father Pixley, therefore, soon determined what he had to do in the affair, to make the circumstances known at the next village; to inquire after the woman, who, no doubt, had been seen either before or after parting with the child; and also to state the whole affair to the nearest justice of the peace.

Within an hour, therefore, after the discovery of the child, the good man might be seen making known his strange news at the different places of resort in the village, and inquiring from all if such a person as the little girl had described the woman to be, had been seen by any; but to his chagrin and amazement, no one could give him information—such a person had evidently not been there. He next hastened to the justice's. It was now evening, and Walter Pixley was informed that his worship very rarely transacted any business after dinner, and that especially "he would not with a Quaker." Walter, however, was not easily to be put by; he felt his business was important, and, by help of a gratuity to the servant, he gained admittance.

The justice was engaged over his wine, and he received Walter Pixley very gruffly, and in the end threatened him with a committal to jail for his pains. The poor Quaker had been in jail the whole of the preceding winter, and he remembered too wofully the horror of that dungeon to bring upon himself willingly a second

M

incarceration. It was of no use seeking for help at the hands of the justice, therefore he urged his business no further, and returned quietly to his own house.

Against the will, therefore, of the elder Pixleys, the child was established with them; and it was not long before the father and mother as cordially adopted it as their little daughter had done from the first beholding it. "For who knows," argued the good Walter Pixley, "but the child may be designed for some great work, and therefore removed thus singularly from the ways of evil, for our teaching and bringing up? Let us not gainsay or counteract the ways of Providence." This reasoning abundantly satisfied the pious minds of the good Friends, and the little stranger was regularly installed a member of the family by the kindred name of Mary.

At the time little Mary was first received under this hospitable roof, she might be about six months old, a child of uncommon beauty; nor, as the months advanced into years, was the promise of her infancy disappointed. She was, in disposition and tone of mind, the very reverse of her grave and gentle elder sister, as Martha

was now considered; she was bold and full of
mirth; full of such unbroken buoyancy of heart
as made the sober mother Pixley half suspect
that she must have come of some race of wild
people. Certain it was, the subdued and grave
spirit of the Pixleys never influenced her, and
as Martha grew up into womanhood, and the
quietness and sobriety of her younger years
matured into fixed principle, she embraced with
a firm mind the peculiar tenets in which she
had been brought up, and would have stood to
the death for the maintenance of them. Mary
also advanced past the years of girlhood, but
still remained the gay, glad, bold-spirited being
that she had ever been. She revered all the members of the persecuted body to whom her friends
belonged, and would have suffered fearlessly for
their sakes; still, their principles and practices
she never would adopt. Her beautiful person
was adorned, as far as she had opportunity, in
the prevailing fashion of the time; and she
often grieved the sober minds of every member
of the family by carolling forth "profane songs,"
as Mrs Pixley called them; while how she
became acquainted with them remained for ever
a mystery. Often did the conscientious mind

of Father Pixley question with himself, whether
it was quite right to maintain so light a maiden
under his roof; but then the affectionate being,
who had no friends save them in the world, had
so entwined herself round the hearts of all the
household, that the good man banished the idea
as inhuman, and never ventured to give it utterance. Martha and her mother, meantime,
strove to win over this bright young creature
to their own views, and for a few moments she
would settle her beautiful face to a solemn
expression, try to subdue what her friends called
" her airy imagination," and attend the preaching
of some eminent Friend. But it would not do—
the true character burst forth through all—
Mary was again all wit and laughter, and
though her friends reproved, they loved her,
and forgave all.

On the accession of James II., which is the
period at which our little narrative is now
arrived, persecution raged again with greater
violence than ever ; and the Pixleys, along
with seventeen other Friends, both men and
women, were dragged from their meeting-house
by a brutal soldiery, under the command of
the justice we have before mentioned, to the

dungeon-like county jail, in the depth of winter. The hardships they endured were so dreadful, that it is painful to relate them. They were kept many days without food, and allowed neither fire nor candle; their prison was damp and cold, and they were furnished with straw only for their beds; they were also forbidden to see their friends, who might have procured them some of the necessaries of life; nor were they allowed to represent, by letter, their case to any influential man of the county, who might have interested himself in their behalf. And to all this was added the brutality of a cruel jailer, who heaped upon them all the ignominy he could devise. In these dreadful circumstances lay the gentle Martha Pixley and her parents. Mary, not having accompanied them to their place of worship, did not share their fate.

Poor Mother Pixley's health had long been declining, and this confinement reduced her so low that in a few days her life was despaired of; still, no medical aid could be procured, and the cloaks and coats of many of her suffering companions were given up to furnish covering for her miserable bed.

When the news came to Mary of the

committal of her friends to jail, the distress of her
mind expressed itself in a burst of uncontroll-
able indignation; and then, asking counsel of
no one, she threw on her hat and cloak, and
taking with her an old man who lived in the
family as a labourer, she hurried to the justice's; and, as she did not appear with any
mark of the despised Quaker, either in dress or
manner, she soon obtained admittance. The
magistrate was somewhat startled by the sudden
apparition of so fair and young a maiden, and
demanded her pleasure with unwonted courtesy,
seating her in the chair beside him, and removing from his head the laced hat which he was
wearing at her entrance. Mary made her
demand for the liberation of her friends, the
Quakers. The justice stared, as if doubting his
senses, and rallied her on the strangeness of her
request, charging upon the Quakers all those
absurd and monstrous things which were alleged
against them in those days. Mary, nothing
abashed, denied every charge as false, and
demanded, if not the liberation of her friends,
at least the amelioration of their sufferings.
As Mary pleaded, the justice grew angry, and
at length the full violence of his temper broke

forth, and the high-spirited girl, even more indignant than terrified, rushed from his presence.

What was next to be done? She ordered her old attendant to saddle the horses, and mounting one, and bidding him follow on the other, she set off to the county town. There she found great numbers of Friends surrounding the prison with baskets of provisions, bedding, warm clothing, and fuel, begging for admittance to their perishing brethren. Little children, too, there were, weeping for their imprisoned parents, and offering their little all to the jailer, so that they might be permitted to share their captivity. Mary made her way through this melancholy crowd, peremptorily demanded access to the jailer, and was admitted, her garb, unlike that of the persecuted Quakers, obtaining for her this favour, as at the house of the justice. But here again her errand debarred her further success; the jailer would neither allow her to see her friends, nor would he convey a message to them. Mary could have wept in anger and vexation, and from intense sympathy with the grief she had witnessed outside the walls, but she did not; she retorted upon the jailer the

severity of his manner, and, bidding him look
to the consequences, folded her cloak round her,
and walked forth again into the circle of Friends
who surrounded the gate. The jailer laughed
as he drew the heavy bolts after her, and bade
her do her worst.

Among the Friends collected in the street
before the prison, Mary heard that William
Penn, who had just returned from his new settlement in America, was now in London. As
soon as she heard this, she determined upon her
plan of conduct. She knew his influence with
the king, who, when Duke of York, had induced
his brother, Charles II., to bestow on him that
tract of land called Pennsylvania. To him,
therefore, she determined to go, and pray him
to represent to the king the deplorable sufferings
of Friends in those parts.

When her old attendant heard of her medi-
tated journey, he looked upon her as almost
insane. To him the project was appalling. It
would require many days to reach London,
and who must take charge of the farm in his
absence, seeing his worthy master was in prison?
And then, too, though he had been willing to
attend her as far as the next town, would it be

right for a young maiden and an old man to
endanger their lives by so long and so strange
a journey?

Mary was uninfluenced by his reasoning, nor
was she to be daunted by his fears. " If," she
said, " he would not accompany her, she would
go alone." She bade him, therefore, to have
her horse saddled by break of day, and retired
to her own apartment, to · prepare for the
journey.

" Of a surety," said the old man to himself,
"she is a wilful young thing."

In the morning, however, she found not only
her horse prepared, but the old man and his
also, for wilful as she was, the old man loved
her; and though he could not conjecture the
object of so strange a journey, " he would," he
said, " go with her to the end of the world."

Mary had ventured to make use of the stores
in Walter Pixley's coffers, for she considered
the lives of her friends were at stake. She was,
therefore, sufficiently supplied with money for
their journey.

For this time the wild gaiety of Mary's spirits
was gone, but instead, was a strong energy and
determination of character, which supported

her above fatigue, or the apprehension of danger; and day after day, from town to town, in the depth of winter, did she and her attendant journey onward. They had no intercourse with travellers on the road, nor did they make known to any one the object of their journey.

When she arrived in London she went straight to the house where William Penn had his temporary residence, and without introduction, apology, or circumlocution, laid before that great and good man the sad condition of her suffering friends. She then made him acquainted with her own private history, her obligations to the family of the worthy Walter Pixley, and the anxiety she now felt for the life of her who had been as a mother unto her.

William Penn heard her with evident emotion, and promised to do all that lay in his power for her benefactors; though he assured her she had overrated his influence with the king. He then desired Mary to take up her abode under his roof; and bidding an attendant call in his mistress, he gave her into the hands of his fair and gentle wife, briefly relating to her on what errand the maiden had come.

When Mary found her mission thus far so

happily accomplished, and the door shut upon herself and her kind hostess, the overstrained energy of her spirit for a moment relaxed, and she wept like a feeble child. The fair wife of William Penn understood her feelings, soothed her with sympathy, and encouraged her to open her heart freely. Never had Mary seen goodness so graceful and attractive as in the high-minded and gentle being before her. Her very soul blessed her as she spoke; she could not doubt but that all would be well; and with her heart comforted, assured, and filled with gratitude, it seemed as if a new life had been given to her.

The next day William Penn obtained an audience of the king, and so wrought upon him by the story of the heroic young creature under his roof, and the sufferings of her friends, that he desired she might be brought before him, and receive from his own hands the order for their enlargement.

Mary was accordingly arrayed in the best garments her scanty wardrobe permitted, by the elegant and gentle hands of Gulielma Penn, who surveyed her beautiful face and figure with admiration, and then kissed her and blessed

her, as an affectionate mother might bless a
beloved daughter.

Leaning upon the arm of her protector, she
was conducted through a great chamber of lords
and ladies, assembled for the occasion, into the
presence of his majesty. Mary's heart beat
violently as her companion, drawing her arm
from his, presented her to his sovereign, who
graciously bade her speak her wishes without
fear. Re-assured by the kindness of the king's
manner, almost forgetting the presence in which
she stood for what seemed to her the greater
importance of her errand, she made her petition
gracefully and well. She related all she had
told William Penn of the great kindness of the
Pixleys to her, and her otherwise desolate condition; she told of their domestic virtues, of
their piety, and their firm loyalty; and lastly,
of their wretched condition in the jail, with that
of many others, and of the cruelty of the justice
and the jailer; and then, almost unconsciously
falling on her knees, she prayed so eloquently
that they might be released, that the king
turned aside to wipe away a tear before he put
forth his hand to raise her.

The petition was granted. The king himself

put into her hands the order for their release, and then praying God might bless her, and taking leave of William Penn very kindly, passed out of the presence-chamber. Many of the lords accompanied the king, but the rest, closing around the almost terrified maiden, over-whelmed her with compliments. William Penn, who saw her confusion, apologised for her with all the grace of a courtier, and extricating her from the admiring company, conveyed her, like a being walking in a dream, to his own house.

Not a moment was lost in sending down by express the order for the Friends' enlargement, and together with that, a dismissal from his office for the jailer. Rest was now absolutely necessary for Mary after these extraordinary exertions; William Penn detained her, there-fore, a few days under his roof, and then con-veyed her himself in his own comfortable carriage to the house of her friends. It is impossible to describe the joy which her return afforded, and which was not a little increased by the presence of her illustrious companion.

The troubles and persecutions of the Pixleys here came to an end, for they went over to Pennsylvania with its distinguished founder, on his return, and became noted among the most worthy and influential of the settlers there. Mary, however, returned to England, being affluently married; and I, myself, several years ago, was possessed of a piece of needle-work said to have been of her doing.

A COTTAGE MEMOIR.

A COTTAGE MEMOIR.

Elizabeth Brown, or, as she was always called at home, Bessy, was ten years old when we shall first introduce her to our readers. She could at this time knit, sew, and read; she could also write a little, and cast accounts rather less—in fact, she could just add an easy addition sum, and tell how many farthings make a penny, how many pence a shilling, and how many shillings a guinea, a pound, or a sovereign. She knew, moreover, the church catechism, the ten commandments, the Lord's prayer, a few hymns, and a few songs, the names and order of the twelve months, the number of days in a year, and that she was born in the year 1815; and consequently, in the year 1825, the time at which we are arrived, she was ten years old.

N

With this small stock of learning, she was
nevertheless a happy child, and was tractable
and useful in her father's house. ‐ She could
wash the floor, prepare the small meals of the
family, put the dinner things aside, rub the
tables and chairs, and then carry out the baby
into the sunshiny fields, without endangering
it either in life or limb. She was a great help
to her mother, who, when fretted by having to
provide for a large family out of the scanty
earnings of her husband, a labouring-man,
used sometimes to scold her for playing at hop-
scotch and burn-ball with the neighbouring
children, when she wanted her to mend stockings and nurse the baby; yet, at the same time,
she internally admitted her good little daughter's usefulness, and often said to herself, that
she should be at her wits' end without the help
of little Bessy.

Bessy was a strong girl of her age, rather
robust than tall, and was brown with being
exposed to all weathers; her hair was parted in
front and put behind her ears, and turned up
behind into a little knot with a sixpenny comb
which she had bought at the last fair. She wore
dark cotton frocks, made up to the neck, but

with short sleeves, because her mother said it
saved stuff, and was more convenient for
washing and cleaning; excepting, however, her
Sunday frock of smart pink and green print,
which had long ones, and in which Bessy felt
herself in full dress. She wore a stuff petticoat,
black worsted stockings, and thick shoes;
indeed, she was the pattern of a tidy, little old
woman. When she went to the town, she had
on a black bonnet, made out of an old mode
cloak of her grandmother's, and a cotton shawl
in which she folded her gloveless arms. She
could make a very good bargain for potatoes,
but with the purchase of the little piece of meat
intended for the Sunday dinner, she was not
intrusted, being, as her mother said, too young
and too inexperienced to be employed in a
matter of such importance. She, however,
bought the flour, and made the bread, which
was an accomplishment she took as much pride
in as many a fashionable young lady does in the
execution of a difficult piece of music, or the
painting of a smart pair of hand-screens; and
this bread she carried to the bakehouse and
fetched back again; and soon grew a connois-
seur in loaves, and could tell at a glance which

would be light and which heavy, and which, like her own, would be very excellent bread indeed.

People who were out early in the morning, used to see Bessy Brown, with her frock pinned up, in a pair of pattens, with a little canvas apron, mopping the red bricks of the floor, and the pavement before their cottage door. About half-past twelve she was again outside the door, but at the end of the house by a bench under the great pear-tree, with a round iron pot filled with hot water, and a wooden lid, with a nail driven into it for a handle, standing beside her, washing up the dinner things. In an afternoon, which was Bessy's holiday-time, she might be seen wandering out with the baby in her arms, in its cotton bonnet and blue handkerchief, into the pleasant fields, gathering buttercups and daisies for her little charge, or blackberries for herself; or else sitting on the grass, or at the house door, singing and talking, and putting herself into all sorts of odd, entertaining atti- tudes, to amuse the infant; and then again in an evening, when it was wearied out, she rocked it to sleep, and gave it to the mother for the night; or else, as it grew older, took it to her own little bed, and even in her deep and healthy slumbers watched over it with a love as true and tender as that of a mother.

One day of Bessy's life was a sample of her days for four years; for, as one baby grew into a chubby child that ran about independently and amused itself, another little brother or sister succeeded to its place, and kept her always nursing. But when she was fourteen years old, her mother began to think it was time that Bessy was earning her own living; and, as her next daughter was growing up, and was able to take Bessy's place in the house, she began to inquire if any family in the neighbourhood wanted a tidy girl to help in the kitchen, or take care of a child.

There seemed something very pleasant and independent to the little girl's mind at first, in the idea of going to service; she thought of the wages she should get, of the things she should buy; talked of it all day, and dreamed of it all night. At length a place was found—she was to be little nurse-maid at the Green Dragon, in her native village.

Her mother thought that they should see Bessy very often, and how they should pass the door every Sunday, as they went to church; and

besides, Mrs Martin was reckoned a very good
sort of woman, and would, she did not doubt,
prove a kind mistress ; and the baby, though a
great heavy boy, to be sure, had a little yellow
coach to ride in, and Bessy could draw him up
the road to their cottage, as well as any other
way, and might perhaps meet her father or one
of her brothers, and they should thus have a
chance of news of her during the week. And,
though the landlord of the Green Dragon was a
stern man, a very dragon himself in temper, it
was well known that Mrs Martin had the management of the whole establishment, including
men and maids ; and, therefore, poor Mrs Brown
persuaded herself that it was very well for a
first place, as times went.

It was accordingly agreed upon by all parties.
Although Bessy's aspirings were a little humbled
in living *only* at the Green Dragon, instead of
the parsonage, or at the 'squire's, as she had
hoped, she tried to fancy it would be very grand
to see the mail-coach stop every morning,
with all its fine passengers and its four fine
horses. On the Monday morning, therefore, it
was fixed that she was to go.

Her poor mother had laid out all the money

she could save, ever since it was concluded that
Bessy was to go to service, in completing her
little wardrobe for the last time; in future she
must supply it herself from her own earnings.
Her few clothes were put in good repair, and
her heart was made to overflow with gratitude
by one present from her poor mother, who felt
more regret in parting with her good little
daughter than she chose to express—and that
present was her own white dimity petticoat!
That beautiful garment, as Bessy thought, which
her mother wore and washed once in a summer,
to keep it a good colour, and in which she was
married! The first white petticoat Bessy ever
had possessed, and which was tucked up, and
altered for her own wear: poor Bessy was grateful, even to tears. All her clothes were neatly
put up in a small oaken chest, which, together
with a prayer-book, was her father's present;
and on Sunday evening they sat down to take
their last meal all together—at least for some
time.

This first going out to service is a great event
in the life of the poor; the rich have nothing
like it. It is a practical going forth of a young
creature to seek her fortune, and often a very

hard fortune it turns out ; and Bessy, though a
stout-hearted girl, felt some natural misgivings
of spirit, as to-morrow, with its untried life,
stood before her, at the distance of but a few
hours. Much was the good counsel given to
her by her simple-hearted parents this evening ;
and many the warnings drawn from the experience of her mother, who herself had lived fourteen years in various services. The supper-
things stood long unmoved from the little table
before Bessy could find courage to put them
away, as she said to herself, "for the last time."

Her sleep this night was less profound than
usual ; and, for the first time in her life since
the baby died, she awoke with a depression of
spirits. Long and tearful was the leave-taking
between her and her mother and the little ones
before she had the courage to follow her father,
who, laden with her worldly possessions, was
waiting to accompany her to the Green Dragon
—to conduct her, as it were, across the thresh-
old on her entrance into life.

Bessy's first place was a very hard one. The
child was cross, heavy, and spoiled ; she had to
nurse him, to obey the petulant, fat landlord,
and to wait on the impatient Mrs Martin and

her twenty guests at the same moment. The
child would not be drawn up the road in his
yellow coach, nor would Mrs Martin allow her
to speak to her parents at the door, as they
passed on their way to church. Poor girl! she
began to think service was very hard, and to
remember, with almost painful pleasure, the
happy days of wandering in the fields with her
good little baby-brother, when she used to peep
into birds' nests and gather black-berries. Many
a time did she cry herself to sleep; but then she
remembered that her mother's first service had
been hard also; that she lived with a mistress
who had even beaten her; and therefore she
supposed that it was all in the order of things
for "first places" to be bad ones, and she
endured her troubles without complaint.

Bessy, however, stayed only twelve months at
the Green Dragon. She had been seen by the
draper of the next town, as, in making his
rounds among his country customers, he had
stopped at the Green Dragon, and had recom-
mended her to his wife as the neatest, quickest-
handed little maiden he had ever seen. Therefore, when she was out of place, she was hired
by the lady in question as an attendant upon

her smart little daughter, just turned three years of age.

But, in the twelve months of Bessy's hard servitude, she had gone through a useful discipline; she had strengthened her mind by patience and forbearance, and her unparticipated sorrows, if for a time they had made her a sadder, had in the end assuredly made her a wiser girl. She had also grown much taller and fairer, and had altogether a more trim, cultivated look. Her small wages had been laid out in the supplying her wardrobe with better apparel; her hair had lost its sun-burned look, had now grown long, and was put up with some degree of taste, and she wore long-sleeved gowns in an afternoon, and white cotton stockings on a Sunday. Bessy was certainly bidding fair to be a very comely young maiden.

She lived at the draper's for four years; and then she was nineteen years old, and wore caps and frills, and had a silk shawl, a variety of printed gowns, and blue ribbons in her bonnet; besides this, she had four pounds in money saved out of her earnings, a smart red-leather housewife, a paper work-box, and a silver thimble. Poor Bessy! she began to feel how pleasant it was to have some little property of her own. After she had lived four years at the draper's, Miss Mary Ann was sent to a boarding-school, and her services were no longer wanted either to accompany the little girl in her walks, or to get-up her white muslin dresses when they were washed; Bessy was therefore again out of place.

This latter, unlike Bessy's first situation, had been one of comparative ease; for her mistress, who loved and lived in all bodily comforts herself, took care that her servants, were it only for the credit of the house, should not have great cause of complaint; nevertheless, she was a cross-tempered, exact woman, and her servants obeyed her as much in fear as love. Still, Bessy always thought herself extremely well-off; she had been indulged with a journey to the sea-side when her mistress and Miss Mary Ann went there for the benefit of sea-bathing, and had always the reputation of being a favourite in the family. Occasional troubles, it is true, Bessy had, but these left no unpleasant memories behind, and she parted from her mistress with tears in her eyes and a true sorrow at her heart; in return, she received, as a parting present, a gown of one of the best prints in her master's shop.

When, on leaving this place, Bessy paid a visit to her parents, and in her very best apparel, a tall, comely young woman, made her first appearance at church, all her old companions looked upon her as a person whose acquaintance would be very creditable to them. Her mother, too, with a very pardonable pride, when the service was over, stopped on purpose that the clergyman and his wife might see her.

A proud and happy woman was she, when they acknowledged her deep curtsey, and that of the daughter, with a very gracious smile, of which she gave half the credit to Bessy's respectable appearance. The squire's lady, too, waited to see them pass, and then turned and spoke to her handsome daughter, something which Mrs Brown was sure, in her own mind, was to Bessy's advantage—and the poor woman walked home, the happiest mother in the whole congregation. "I always thought she would be a credit to us," she said to herself; "such a tidy, notable girl! I hope Mary, and Jane, and little Sarah, will turn out as well!"

The next day, to the great joy of Bessy's

mother, the clergyman's pony-chaise stopped at their cottage-door, and in a few minutes his lady entered to make inquiries respecting her. If she could have a good character from her last place, she said she could offer her a situation in her own family. Bessy's good conscience assured her, in a moment, all would be right; and blushing, and full of ill-concealed joy, she thanked the kind lady for the offer a thousand times. A favourable character was soon received from her late mistress, and in two weeks' time the dream of Bessy's childhood was realised, and she and her personal property, now occupying two tolerably large paper trunks, besides the little oaken chest before mentioned, were removed to the beautiful parsonage. Here she lived five years, a happy and respectable servant, fulfilling every duty, and with a conscience void of offence; and at the end of that time only left it to be married to her fellow-servant, the gardener, as steady and industrious a young man as even Mrs Brown herself could desire for her dutiful daughter.

THE HONEST DUTCHMAN.

IT came to pass, in the
days of old, that the men of Holland
found themselves straitened in their
habitations; for who knows not that
they were, from the first, a sober,
hardy, and industrious race, tilling
the ground, buying and selling, eating
and drinking in humility, and therefore they

lived to a good old age, and "sent forth their little ones like a flock, and their children danced;" so that their land being small, they filled it brimful of inhabitants, till they were ready to overflow all its borders. And they looked this way, and that way, and they said: "What shall we do, for the people are many, and the land is small, and we are much straightened for room?" So they called together the chief men of their nation, and they held a great council to consider what they must do. And behold, there arose amongst them a man unlike the men of the land, for they were short, and broad, and well-formed in body, of a solemn and quiet countenance, and clad in peaceable garments; but he was tall and bony, and of a grim and hairy aspect. He had a great hard hand and a fierce eye; his clothes had a wild look; he had a sword by his side, a spear in his grasp, and his name was Van Manslaughter.

With a glad but a savage gaze, he looked round upon the assembly, and said: "Fellow-citizens! I marvel at your perplexity. You sit quietly at home, and know nothing of the world; but I and my followers have pursued the deer and the boar far away into the forests of Germany. We have fought with the wolf and the bear, and, if need were, with the men of the woods; and enjoy our hunting, and eat of our prey with joy and jollity. Why sit ye here in a crowd, like sheep penned in a fold? We have seen the land that is next to ours, and we have been through it, to the length of it and to the breadth of it, and it is a good land. There are corn and wine: there are cities, towns, and villages ready built to our hands. Let us arise and come suddenly upon them, and we shall not only get all these possessions, but we shall get great glory." And when he had so said, he looked round him with much exultation, and a crowd of dark hairy faces behind him cried out: "Ay, it is true! Let us arise and get great glory!"

But at that word there stood up Mynheer Kindermann, an old man—a very old man. He was of low stature, of a stout broad frame, and his hair, which was very white, hung down upon his shoulders; and his beard also, as white as driven snow, fell reverently upon his breast. That old man had a large and tranquil countenance; his features were bold, and of a very healthful complexion; his face, though of a goodly breadth, was of a striking length, for his forehead was bold and high, and his eyes had a pleasant fireside expression, as though he had been used only to behold his children and his children's children at their play, or to fix them on the loving forms of his wife or his friend. As he arose there was a great silence, and he stood and sighed; and those who were near him heard him mutter in a low tone the word "Glory," but those afar off only saw his lips move. Then he said aloud: "My brethren! I am glad that you are called upon to get great glory, but what is that glory to which Mynheer Van Manslaughter calls you? In my youth, as some of you well know, I travelled far and wide with my merchandise; I have sojourned in all the countries that adjoin ours, and they are truly good countries, and full of people; but what of that? It is not people that we lack, it is land; and I should like to know how we are to take this land, that is full of people, and yet do those people no wrong! If we go to take that land, we shall find the people ready to defend their homes and their children; and if we fight in a bad cause, we shall probably get

beaten, like thieves and robbers, for our pains—
and is that glory? But if we are able to take
that land, we must first kill or drive out those
that cultivate it, and make it fit to live in—and
is that glory? And if we take those cities, and
towns, and villages, we must kill those who
built them, or have lived pleasantly in them,
with God's blessing. Oh! what honest, inoffen-
sive men, what good, kind-hearted mothers,
what sweet and tender brothers and sisters,
what dear little babes we must murder and
destroy, or drive away from their warm homes
which God has given them, and which are
almost as dear to them as their lives, into the
dismal forests, to perish with cold and hunger,
or to be devoured by wild beasts, and, in their
anguish, to curse us before the Great Father
who made us all! My brethren, I cannot think
that is glory, but great disgrace and infamy,
and a misery that, I trust, shall never come
upon us.

"I have long looked about me, and I see
that Heaven has given all those countries round
us to whom He would, and they are full of
people; they are full of rich fields and vine-
yards; they are full of towns for men and

temples for God ; they are full of warm, bright,
happy homes, where there are proud fathers,
and glad mothers, and innocent children, as
amongst ourselves; and cursed be he who would
disturb or injure them !

" But, my brethren, how shall we get glory,
and, what is of more immediate necessity, how
shall we get land to live in ? I have been thinking of this, and it has come into my mind that
it has been too long the custom for men to call
themselves *warriors* when they desire to be
murderers, and to invade the property and the
lives of their neighbours; and I have thought,
as all the land is taken up, and as we cannot
without great sin invade the land, that *we had
better invade the sea*, where we can take, and
wrong no man ! And who does not know, that
has looked towards the sea, that there is much
ground which seems properly to belong neither
to the sea nor the land ? Sometimes it is
covered with the waters, and sometimes it is
partly bare—a dreary, slimy, and, profitless
region, inhabited only by voracious crabs that
make war upon one another—the stronger upon
the weaker—and sea-fowl which come in like
conquerors and subdue them, and devour them,

and get what Van Manslaughter calls 'great glory!' My brethren, let us invade the sea— let us get piles, and beams, and stones, and dig up the earth, and make a large mound which will shut out the sea, and we shall have land enough and to spare."

As he finished his speech there arose a deep murmur that grew and grew till it spread among the people collected in thousands without, and at length became like the sound of the ocean itself; and then the people cried out, "Yes, we will invade the sea!" and so it was decreed. Then began they with axes to fell wood; with levers and mattocks to wrench up stones ; and with wagons, horses, and oxen, to lead them to the sea. Now, it being the time of low-water, and the tide being gone down very far, they began to dig up the earth and to make a mighty bank. So when the sea came up again, it saw the bank and the people upon it in great numbers, but it took no notice thereof. And it went down and came up again, and they had pushed out the bank still further, and raised it higher, and secured it with beams, and piles, and huge stones, and it began to wonder. And it went down and came up again, and they had

pushed the bank still further, so that in great
amaze it said within itself: "What are these
insignificant creatures doing? Some great
scheme is in their heads, but I wot not what;
and one of these days I will come up and over-
turn their bank, and sweep both it and them
away together." But, at length, as it came up
once on a time, it beheld that the bank was
finished. It stretched across from land to land,
and the sea was entirely shut out. Then was
it filled with wonder that such little creatures
had done so amazing a deed, and with great
indignation that they had presumed to interrupt
the progress of itself—the mighty sea, which
stretched round the whole world, and was the
greatest moving thing in it. Retreating in fury,
it collected all its strength, and came with all
its billows, and struck the bank in the midst as
with thunder. In a moment there appeared on
the top of the mound, on the whole length of it,
a swarm of little stout men, thick as a swarm
of bees. Marvellous was it to see how that
throng of little creatures was all astir, running
here and running there; stopping up crevices,
and repairing damages done by that vast and
tremendous enemy, that, roaring and foaming,

repeated its blows like the strokes of a million of battering-rams, till the faces of the men were full of fear, and they said, "Surely the mound will fall!" Then came the sea, swelling and raging more dreadfully than ever, and, urged by the assistance of a mighty wind, it thundered against the bank and burst it! The waters flowed triumphantly over all their old places, and many men perished.

Then went Van Manslaughter amongst the people with great joy, and many loud words, saying: "See what has come of despising my counsel! See what glory your old counsellor has brought you to! Come now, follow me, and I will lead you to possessions where you need not fear the sea. Let us leave it to people this bog with fish. I am for no new-fangled schemes, but for the good old plan of fair and honourable war, which has been the highway to wealth and glory from the beginning of the world."

Then began the people to be very sad, and to listen to his words; but Mynheer Kindermann called them again to him and bid them be of good heart, and to repair the bank, to make it stronger, and to build towers upon it, and to

234

THE HONEST DUTCHMAN.

appoint men to dwell in them that they might continually watch over and strengthen it. So the people took courage and did so, for they said, "Let us take no man's goods, and let us do no murder." Therefore they renewed the mound, and the sea came up in tenfold wrath and smote it worse than before; but it was all in vain. It failed not, save a little here and there, and the people seeing it set up a great shout, and cried: "The mound will stand!"

Then did they begin to dig and drain, to plant trees, to build towns, and to lay out gardens, and it became a beautiful country. Then the inhabitants rejoiced, saying: "Others have invaded lands and killed people, but we have hurt no man. We have only invaded the sea, and Heaven has made us out of it a good heritage!"

These are the people whose wealth and industry are known through the whole world. They have sent out colonies to the ends of the earth, and have got themselves the name of the Honest Dutchmen. Would that they had always been as wise and merciful as they were on that day!   W. H.

THE TALE OF A TRIANGLE.

PART I.

HOW EVIL WAS DONE THAT GOOD MIGHT
COME OF IT.

At a great public school, conducted by the
learned Dr Reader, and many ushers and

masters of many varieties and branches of
knowledge, there were three notable boys. The
tallest boy in the school, the least boy in the
school, and the fattest boy in the school;
Charles, Harry, and George, who, from their
remarkable names of Salmon, Lion, and Sparrow,
were jestingly called, Fish, Flesh, and Fowl.
They had nomen, prenomen, and cognomen.
Charles was also called King, because he was
above his fellows; Harry, Lord, because he
possessed the fat of the land; and George,
Commons, because of his spare person and somewhat meagre aspect. Others, again, distinguished them as Thread-paper, Apple-dumpling,
and Lean Kine. They, however—there being a
sworn league of amity amongst them—had
given themselves the title of " The Triangle ; "
we, therefore, will adopt their own appellation,
and thus style them. So much for their names.

Now, the Triangle, besides their remarkable
exteriors, possessed rare accomplishments ; they
were the best sliders, kite-flyers, top-spinners,
and cricketers in the school. They had, moreover, each his own peculiar gift, which was exercised for general edification. Charles Salmon,
the tall boy, had a wonderful talent for singing;

his voice was clear, melodious, and full of power
and expression, and his performances in this
way, often electrified the whole playground,
when the learned head of Dr Reader himself,
in his white wig, has been seen popping out of
the study-window with an air of abstraction, or
else nodding time to the tune; while it was
very shrewdly conjectured, especially by those
who had seen them, that many an usher like-
wise sought out such commodious nooks and
corners as would give him the enjoyment of
the melody without making him visible to the
urchin crew over whom he exercised authority.

Henry Lion, the. lean boy, was a prodigious
mimic, and acted with inimitable humour every
whimsical character, from Punch to Sir John
Falstaff, to whom, however, he was in bulk a
singular contrast. Nevertheless, he contrived
by some cunning of his own, to swell himself
forth, and appear no Jack Straw in the performance.

The talent of George Sparrow was that of
tale-telling. A very Scheherazade was he in
this accomplishment. Grave or gay, horrible,
fantastical, or pathetic, George Sparrow had a
tale for all times and humours. Happy was the

boy who was his bedfellow, to whom he would
tell tales till the morning bell rang: and yet it
must be confessed to his shame, that into one
little fellow, who had for three months this
honour, he instilled so much terror by his tales
of ghosts, hobgoblins, and bloody murders, that
he fell into what is called a low way, and only
recovered by the intervention of his mother,
who took him home and nursed him for a whole
winter.

Other circumstances made the Triangle not
less remarkable than respectable; they had
never known the infliction of chastisement from
either cane or ferula. Each had been at school
three years, and though they came from different counties, had all entered the same day.
They had all gone honourably and speedily
forward with their school-learning, each first in
some particular branch of knowledge; so that
with mathematical, classical, and English tutors,
as with the head-master himself, they stood
high in estimation. It was a singular Triangle,
all the three sides so various, yet, as a whole,
according so perfectly; and it may be questioned, whether ever a friendship was formed
between two persons, but assuredly, seldom

among three, in which there was a greater unity
of purpose and affection. They were the David
and Jonathan—the Orestes and Pylades of the
school; and from the solemn Dr Reader himself
down to the little Hans Fuggenfelt, the Dutch
boy, who was the most ineffable blockhead in
the school, everybody gave them fair words and
favour.

So stood the Triangle after the midsummer
holidays, when a great boy, half-knave and
half-dunce—one Nathaniel, or, as he was commonly called, Nat Simpkins—became a scholar,
and according to his abilities, which were prodigious in this line, proceeded to set the school
by the ears. The Triangle, being most conspicuous for general favour, was the first object of
his jealousy. He drew a party of weak-minded
boys to his side, and began by artfully insinu-
ating suspicions of underhand proceedings on
the part of the Triangle, plainly expressing his
belief that they were only spared punishment—
corporeal punishment, especially—from the partiality of Dr Reader; while he, the exemplary
Nathaniel Simpkins, who was, according to his
own shewing, superior to them in every respect,
and who had been at the school but two months,

P

had been flogged a dozen times, had learned two
dozen tasks, and had been otherwise publicly
disgraced seventeen times. The thing, he said,
was as plain as daylight, and half the school
began to give him credit for great sagacity in
the discovery. The next thing he did was to
caricature the Doctor, by painting him in his
bag-wig and gown, wearing triangular spec-
tacles, and flogging the whole school with
birch-rod and ferula. This took prodigiously;
any novelty soon wins partisans, and such a
thing as a division, or two sides, in this little
community, was so new, that before many days
were over half the school joined his party, and
were violent accordingly. Simpkins and his
party resolved never to be reconciled to the
Triangulars, till their leaders had undergone
some disgraceful punishment; they therefore
artfully went to work, reproached them with
being *favourites*, and cast endless reflections
on the Doctor for blind partiality. The Triangle
violently resented these reflections on the
Doctor, vindicated him from the charge of
partiality, and maintained that if they or any of
them were worthy of punishment, punishment
they would receive.

"Prove it!—prove it! Shew us that the Doctor is impartial, and we will be friends!" was the reply.

The Triangle were but boys; they meant well, but they argued ill.

"We will prove it!" cried the first.

"We will be the champions of Dr Reader's fair fame!" responded the second.

"We will make ourselves worthy of punishment, to shew you that the good Doctor is incapable of injustice!" echoed the third.

It was at the extremity of the playground, under the dim shade of the old yew-trees, that this singular knight-errantry was sworn, with twenty boys on either side as witnesses. At the conclusion of the ceremony, Arthur Meynell, a firm adherent of the Triangulars, so renowned for the general correctness of his conduct and opinions, that he was commonly surnamed "The Conscience," boldly stepped into the midst, warned the Triangle of their folly and danger, and concluded by saying, that "The Triangle ought to have more sense than to displease the Doctor and disgrace themselves, for a set of idle fellows like those!"

"Coward!—fool!—meddler!—pitiful and

sneaking!"—these were the best words that "The Conscience" got from Simpkins and his party; and the Triangulars were all too busy to listen to him.

The next day the Triangle held a cabinet council, which lasted three hours and three quarters. The result of their deliberations was a plan, according to the best authority, suggested by Sparrow, somewhat improved upon by Salmon, and finally put into accomplishable form by Harry Lion.

What that plan was, and how it was executed, we will proceed to relate.

PART II.

THE HISTORY OF TWO DAYS.

It was a fine September morning, warm and glowing, the harvest was mostly got in, the orchards and gardens were full of beautiful fruit, as the Triangle, having escaped at three o'clock in the morning from an upper window, walked briskly along a wooded lane three miles from the school village.

They had undertaken a three days' ramble round the country, intending nowhere to exceed nine miles distant from the centre, the school; being whimsically determined to direct all their movements in these three days, by their own number. Each boy had three shillings in his pocket; they were to live as merrily as might be, to turn to account each his own peculiar gift in gaining their daily bread and their night's lodging, and what they could not obtain for love, they were to buy for money. At all events, they determined, as far as in them lay, that these three days should be merry ones, come what would afterwards; and all along they made their minds easy by persuading themselves that they were champions in the best cause in the world.

At six o'clock they came to a milkmaid who was singing; from her they obtained a draught of milk, and then proceeded onward, passing through a little town where they bought bread and cheese, upon which they dined. Leaving the town, then, they saw to the right of the road a pleasant hollow overshadowed by trees;

they entered it, and there lying down, Charles
sang *Barbara Allen's Cruelty*, after which they
all three went very comfortably to sleep. When
they awoke, they found the sun beginning to
sink, and, looking round, they saw a farmhouse
below them, half-buried in rich orchard trees,
loaded with bright golden apples. No school-
boy can resist an, apple, and therefore, if they
had not wanted something more substantial,
as they did, they would instinctively have gone
down.

At the door they met a stout, rosy-faced,
loud-spoken dame, stripped to her stays and
green-quilted petticoat, who accosted them
cheerfully. They told her they wanted their
supper and a night's lodging ; she laughed
merrily, and called them "impudent beggars"
and "lazy varlets," and yet said they were
welcome to all her house contained. She then
brought them into the large kitchen, set them
down to a black oak table, and gave them whey
and new bread, fresh-laid eggs and broiled
bacon. It was an excellent feast, they never
had been so hungry in all their lives before,
and never had enjoyed anything half as much.
When they had finished this luxurious meal,

as the good dame had said nothing about the
night's lodging, they rose up to depart, but
she stopped them, saying : " Oh no ! after
such a meal's meat as that, she must have
some work out of them, and therefore they
must stop and help her son in apple-gathering ;"
adding, that " it was lucky they had come, for
if they were only half as ready with their hands
as they had been with their mouths, they would
be a famous help for poor Ned ! "

The Triangle were very well pleased, and
before long poor Ned made his appearance; a
great gawky lad of seventeen, walking like a
cart-horse, and looking as shamefaced as an
owl in the sunshine when he saw the three
" young gentlemen " whom his mother proposed
to him as his associates in the apple-gathering.
The apple-gathering, however, soon made them
very good friends, and then they were merry
altogether ; merry in the orchard ; merry, too, in
the house, into which they carried baskets full
and bags full, bags full and baskets full of the
most delicious apples, until the good dame
herself was tired of reckoning them ; she all
the while laughing and talking, praising the Triangle, praising the apples, and praising her Ned.

After this labour, or rather pastime, and a second hearty supper of roasted apples and new milk, they all sat down by the great kitchen fire, which was made of logs laid on the hearth ; and a jovial party they were ! There was the dame ; poor Ned ; his father, a quiet old man, who said nothing at all, and yet seemed to enjoy everything; two round-faced laughing country girls, and two sleepy, slow-footed lads, ten times duller and heavier than poor Ned himself, and the merry Triangle in the midst, singing songs, telling tales, and acting all humorous and whimsical characters whatever. There they sat at nine o'clock at night ; and there they sat at two o'clock in the morning, and then the good woman, who had laughed and cried alternately for so many hours, hurried her three strange guests upstairs into her best chamber, in which were also deposited cheese, spun-flax, fleeces, and woollen wares ; and wishing them a good night's rest, the kind-hearted dame left them to sleep between the blankets, three in a bed.

The Triangle slept as sound as a top. The cock had long done crowing, poor Ned and his father were out in the fields, and the dame and

her maids busy at their household work, when
the Triangle made its way once more into the
spacious kitchen. And then what a breakfast
they had! The supper overnight was nothing
to it! There were milk and coffee, and oat-
cakes and barley-cakes, eggs and honey, wheaten
bread and spice bread, and various sorts of
country dainties, with and without names. Thus
having banqueted, they again set forth; their
merry and kind-hearted hostess leaving her
cheese-pans to see them across the farmyard
and orchard, and over two fields, a croft, and
meadow, before she could make up her mind to
part with them.

"Fortune has hitherto favoured us!" said the
Triangle; "what will be our fate to-day?"

But that day brought a thunder-storm, which
lasted, from the first heavy drops that came
before to the skirts of the storm that came
after, from eleven o'clock till three; and the
poor Triangle, sadly against its will, took shelter
under an oak-tree. Do what he would to pre-
vent it, all sorts of dismal tales of men struck
blind by lightning, and women and children
struck dead with thunderbolts, came into the
head of George, and for his life he could not

help telling them ; so there they stood, expecting every flash of lightning to leave them blind or dead ! But the storm passed over without injuring them, and, excepting being wet to the skin, they were no worse for it.

On, therefore, they proceeded out of the old pasture fields where they had sheltered, into a long, wooded, and pleasant lane, and here they had not gone far before they were overtaken by their quondam school-fellow, Dick Deriton, now called Mr Richard Deriton or the young 'Squire. He was mounted on a fine racer, and was riding gaily along, giving the reins to his horse, and letting it go at its own pace; he checked it, however, when, to his astonishment, he saw his old companions.

" Heyday, Triangle ! what brings you here ?"

It was soon told. Deriton enjoyed the joke amazingly, leaped from his horse, and throwing the reins on its neck, joined them, and the sagacious animal walked leisurely after its master.

" You shall sleep at our house to-night," said Deriton ; " my father is gone to the races, and doesn't return till to-morrow ; so I 'll invite my friends, the Wigton's, and we 'll have for once a merry night of it ! "

"Excellent!" said the Triangle.

"You shall sing songs, and tell tales, and perform comedy," continued Deriton, "and you shall be encored till the house rings!"

And they were encored till the house rang! There they were in the great dining-room, where they had an excellent dinner, the chandeliers lit, the large table drawn to one end for a stage, and steward, butler, groom, stable-boy, gardener, housekeeper, and half-a-dozen women servants, all for audience; and poor little Harry swelled out for Sir John Falstaff, hectoring and killing a hundred men at a blow, when—oh, unlucky mischance!—in came no other than the old 'Squire himself, all fire and fury, swearing and blustering like ten troopers! Here began a second act in the comedy; out hurried one at one door, and another at another; one got behind a screen, and another under a table; and the old asthmatical butler, as ill-luck would have it, behind the chimney-board, where, on account of his terrible cough, which the dust he disturbed set a-going, it was vain to think of concealment.

The storm of thunder and lightning was nothing to the 'Squire's storm of passion; the

Wigtons were sent home instanter, with orders to wait for his invitation before they came again: every servant had orders to leave, from the old steward, who had served the family for fifty years, to the kitchen-girl, who came 'but the day before. Young Deriton was threatened with being disinherited—a threat which had been too often repeated to be much dreaded— and the Triangle locked up in a chamber, with a promise of being sent back in the morning to Doctor Reader, with such a character as the 'Squire thought they deserved. All this being done he sat himself down to his bottle, which he did not leave till twelve o'clock.

The Triangle deliberately consulted on the state of affairs, and thought it best to be stirring early, at least if they could but get their chamber-door unlocked, for the key was at the other side. But they were helped out of this dilemma by young Deriton, who made his appearance in their chamber by daybreak, and bade them begone, giving each of them a small loaf, and praying them to walk softly. The Triangle thought itself very happy when it was safely out at the back-door, and walked hastily forth through the dewy shrubbery, and among the sweet-smelling and aromatic trees and flowers of the garden, and then took leave of the young 'Squire at the park-gate, who, in spite of his assumed carelessness, they could not help suspecting, wished that his father had found them less jocose than they were at his entrance.

PART III.

OF THE THIRD DAY, AND THE END OF THE ADVENTURE.

A LITTLE sobered, perhaps, with the catastrophe of the last evening, the Triangle walked on over hills and by wood-sides, and across a wide open common, crimsoned with the beautiful heath-flowers, and along the hollows of which ran a bright living rivulet, murmuring like a sweet voice, and glittering in the sunshine. The Triangle went across the heath, and by the water-side, before meeting with any adventure, or seeing anything more extraordinary than the brisk little furze wren, and the green and golden beetles of the common, and the quick-darting trouts, that were seen for a moment and then gone, in the clear water of the beautiful little brook. At the other end of the common stood a small hamlet, which they entered, and where they purchased a good supply of provisions, for after all this rambling in the fresh morning air, they were hungry enough. Leaving the village, they struck into some quiet retired fields, in every one of which stood a new haystack, and seating themselves under one of them, which stood in the prettiest sylvan nook imaginable, they began to discuss the contents of their wallet.

Now it happened, that about two fields' distance from the place where they sat, and directly opposite to it, were three little hills; and, as their eyes were ever on the watch for occasion of merriment, or for subjects of curious speculation, they beheld three men standing, one upon each of these eminences, evidently looking around them in quest of something. North, south, east, and west, they turned, with spy-glasses in their hands to enable them to perceive any small or distant objects, which they ever and anon applied to their eyes, looking round them with great assiduity. They stood up, clear and distinct in the bright light, the morning sun behind them, and were not for a moment to be mistaken! Mathematical, classical, and English teachers in the renowned school of Dr Reader. Away went the Triangle behind the rick, intending from this post to watch, and, for the present, to elude their pursuers.

In a short time the three men of learning, having satisfied themselves, came down from their elevation, and before long entered the very meadow in which the Triangle lay concealed ; and presently afterwards thus came the words of Rhomboid, the mathematician, as they passed by :

" Twenty-seven miles have I walked; forty-five and a half have I ridden ; at eleven houses, and from a hundred and three persons have I made inquiries ; and yet all *my* labour has been in vain."

" So it is," replied Remus, the master of the classics, " fag in-doors, fag out-of-doors; a schoolmaster's life is like a dog's ! "

" Grumble as you will," rejoined Lemuel Prosody, " I hope they've enjoyed their ramble as much as I've enjoyed mine. Sparrow is a prodigy of learning, and if my good word will save them from a flogging, they shall have it for his sake."

" Now Heaven bless you !" whispered Sparrow, when the three wise men had passed by, unwitting of their auditors.

" They may fag on, poor dogs," said Salmon, "but they'll not hunt us out for all that !"

" There they go," said Lion, " due north, and we'll go south, and meet to-morrow morning at breakfast."

It was now past noon, and the Triangle had entered within the bounds of their occasional rambles, and being three miles from the school, were as near as they deemed it safe to venture. They, therefore, turned on to a wild extent of hilly and open land, the remains of an ancient chase. It was full of deep, quiet hollows, the steep banks of which were covered with tall, green bracken, and crimson betony. No pleasanter place could be imagined for a summer-day stroll than this, and to this they came, and lay down all their lengths in one of its most secluded hollows. After they had lain here for about half an hour, and when Sparrow was in the middle of one of his most diverting stories, they beheld what, to their startled imaginations, appeared no other than the veritable Doctor Reader himself, mounted on a strong gray horse, riding up the hollow directly opposite to them.

It perhaps was cowardly to fly, and yet fly they did, up one hollow, and down another, winding about, so as, if possible, to escape pursuit. The horseman spoke not a word, for, trusting to his strong, well-trained horse, he was sure of the chase. Salmon and Lion cleared the ground like greyhounds, the one helped by length of limb, the other by lightness of body; soon distancing poor Sparrow, who was memorably deficient in these two particulars, and who felt himself already in the clutches of the angry Doctor.

"Stop, you terrified fool!" cried the horseman, suddenly wheeling his horse round so as to intercept Sparrow: "Stop, in the name of common sense, and direct me the way to Wimbleton!"

These words restored Sparrow at once to his senses, and out of breath as he was, he gave the required information, Wimbleton being the village where they had last stopped. The

Q

stranger laughed till he almost bent to his saddle-bow, called him "a cowardly blockhead!" for his pains, and rode briskly back again.

By this time Salmon and Lion had returned to their companion, intending to give themselves up also to justice, expecting to find him, with his hands tied behind his back, laid across the horse, like a sheep taken for slaughter.

Despite now all their endeavours to resist the enemy, a feeling of despondency crept over their spirits. They sat down again, intending to wait till the moon rose before they proceeded home; but no song was sung, no tale told, and, which was strange even to themselves, they sat in silence for a quarter of an hour.

At eleven o'clock that night, either by popping in at the keyhole, or scaling the walls, or walking in at the hall-door in invisible jackets, the Triangle, unknown to the whole household (at least, so it seemed), entered their chamber, and lay down in their respective beds, in which they soundly slept till the morning-bell rang.

"Now, Simpkins," said they, as they entered the room where the boys were drawn up, rank and file, for prayers, waiting the entrance of the

masters—"now, Simpkins, for a proof of the
Doctor's impartiality!"

In came the solemn doctor; in came every
tutor and usher. Not a word was said; prayers
were regularly gone through—a silence like
death followed.

Presently an under-master went out, and
returned with three chains, each having at its
extremities manacles, as if to enclose the wrist
and ankle. Some turned pale, but the Triangle
stood firm, and looked neither ashamed nor
terrified.

"Young gentlemen," said the doctor, addressing the three offenders in a deep, stern
voice—"young gentlemen, you have been three
years under my care, during which time you
have not needed punishment, hardly reproof;
the consequence of this has been, that I boasted
of you publicly and privately; I have honoured
your industry and sobriety; I have held you up
as examples to your companions; I have con-
fided in you: but I have been deceived! Gentlemen, I say it with pain—I have been deceived!
—I can boast of you, I can honour you, I can
confide in you no longer! Is it possible, that
from the favour you have received from me—

and which you only received because you appeared to deserve it—that you supposed I should pass over your delinquencies, or permit you to infringe the laws of order without punishment! Corporeal punishment by stripes, however, you shall not receive at my hands, so far I will still respect your former unblamable conduct; but since you have forfeited my confidence, I must secure your persons, and make you an example to the school.

" You, perhaps, imagine me ignorant of your idle wanderings for these three days; you are mistaken. I know where you have been; what company you have kept; and how you have demeaned yourselves.

" Again, I repeat it, my confidence has been abused, and with deep sorrow I leave you for the present to your own reflections !—Mr Beetham, do your duty."

The fetters were put on, and the Triangle, bound hand and foot, went out, somewhat grave, yet, nevertheless, unsubdued in aspect. As soon as they entered the playground, a stunning shout greeted them from their own party. Doctor Reader was sitting in his little back-parlour, when these sounds of triumph reached him, and very much disconcerted was he to hear them. There was something very unaccountable to him in the whole proceeding. He was mortified and amazed at what seemed to him the obstinate temper of the three offenders, whom, to say the truth, he loved as well, perhaps, as he would have loved children of his own, had he possessed any; and more than this, for the first time in his life, he began to question the power of his own eloquence, or to suspect that his mode of punishment was injudicious, since it produced so strange a result. Grieved, therefore, and a little out of humour, he walked into his study, intending to make silent but exact observation on all that went forward in the playground. Great, therefore, was his amazement, when he beheld the three culprits seated on a platform, and borne upon the shoulders of many boys, while others ran before, waving caps and handkerchiefs, and shouting " Victory ! Victory ! Justice, the good Doctor Reader, and the Triangle for ever !"

The Doctor was more amazed and bewildered than before. He hastened, therefore, to the scene of action, determined to have it explained,

and followed the triumphal procession to the
yew-tree walk, and there found the victors
seated upon a rude sort of throne.

The unexpected appearance of the Doctor
rather disconcerted the Triangle, who, feeling
that this defiance, as it were, of punishment,
might very justly still further displease him,
wished internally that the whole affair was
explained; but as no one of the three did
explain it, Arthur Meynell, otherwise called
" The Conscience," who saw it in the same
light as themselves, stepped forward, and in
an astonishingly short time laid open the whole
plot, declaring that the triumph he now witnessed was only the Triangulars rejoicing that
the justice and impartiality of the good Doctor
was unquestionably established. This being
said, he was so led away by his enthusiasm,
that even in presence of that grave personage
himself, he shouted " Justice, the good Doctor
Reader, and the Triangle for ever! " in which
shout every boy joined, till the poor Doctor
was half-deafened by the uproar

At length, when silence was obtained, with
some severity of countenance, which amazed
his vehement young partisans, he ordered them

quietly to assemble in the school-room. They did so; and then he again harangued them— and not only the Triangle and its party, but Nat Simpkins and his.

The Triangle felt, for the first time, and were not slow to acknowledge it, how improperly and unwisely they had acted; and never, while they remained at school—nay, nor afterwards through the whole course of their lives, did they again " do evil that good might come of it."

THE END.

Edinburgh :
Printed by W. and R. Chambers.

www.ingramcontent.com/pod-product-compliance
Lightning Source LLC
Chambersburg PA
CBHW030352270326
41926CB00009B/1064